PUT THE
DISCIPLE
INTO
DISCIPLINE

PUT THE
DISCIPLE
INTO
DISCIPLINE

Parenting with Love and Limits

Erin MacPherson
and Ellen Schuknecht

FaithWords

NEW YORK   NASHVILLE

FaithWords
Hachette Book Group
1290 Avenue of the Americas, New York, NY 10104
faithwords.com
twitter.com/faithwords

First edition: June 2017

FaithWords is a division of Hachette Book Group, Inc. The FaithWords name and logo are trademarks of Hachette Book Group, Inc.

The publisher is not responsible for websites (or their content) that are not owned by the publisher.

The Hachette Speakers Bureau provides a wide range of authors for speaking events. To find out more, go to www.hachettespeakersbureau.com or call (866) 376-6591.

LCCN 2017003012

ISBNs: 978-1-4789-1809-7 (paperback), 978-1-4789-4786-8 (ebook)

Printed in the United States of America

LSC-C

10 9 8 7 6 5 4 3 2 1

For my three kids:
Joey, Kate, and Will
—Erin

For my precious grandchildren:
Joey, Kate, Jude, Haddassah,
Greta, Will, Isaac, Asa,
Elsie, Alma, and Bethlehem
—Ellen

Contents

Discipline That Disciples

(ELLEN)

I HAVE ELEVEN GRANDCHILDREN, all under the age of ten.

Joey, the oldest, is passionate and curious. Kate is kind and generous. Jude is analytical and pensive. Haddie is outgoing and creative. Greta is witty and engaging. Will is exuberant and courageous. Isaac is brave and hilarious. Asa is compassionate and assertive. Elsie is meticulous and loving. Alma is determined and friendly. And Beth Ellen is joyful and tender.

I could go on and on about each of them for pages...but it's clear in just one paragraph: Each of my grandkids was given a unique, God-given personality. Each of them has incredible strengths—character traits that I pray God will use to truly impact his kingdom. And each of them has some weaknesses—attributes that they must learn to control and overcome if they want to grow into healthy, productive adults.

Yes, each one is different, from the top of their red- or brown- or blond-haired heads to the tips of their sparkle-boot- or soccer-shoe-clad toes. And I know that God created your kids uniquely wonderful, too, each with a special purpose, special plan, and special gifts to boot. Yet, while I think every one of us recognizes these innate differences in our kids, when it comes to discipline, so many of us try to fit our kids into a prescribed plan.

I'll just come out and say it: That doesn't make sense.

I've come to believe that many of the parenting experts got it wrong. I'm not saying that their ideas and tools are wrong—I often refer to my tall stack of parenting books when it comes to discipline—but so many of the common parenting books and touted parenting methods lack one thing: They forget about discipleship. They tell you how to demand obedience and honesty and good behavior but don't cover how to teach our kids to truly desire right and how to show them the love that God so readily (and mercifully) pours out on us.

Erin and I want to change that.

We're not telling you to throw out all of your discipline books. We're asking you to consider the idea that maybe discipline is a bit bigger than what you've thought it was. While it may take a bit more work, by focusing on discipleship and heart connection, you can create a lasting bond with your kids that runs deep—and helps your kids to truly see Jesus's love in a tangible way. Maybe when your kids mess up, it is a chance for their hearts to be refined by God and moved toward Him.

Before we get to the good stuff—we're going to take you through several real discipline scenarios from real parents— I thought it would be a good idea to lay a foundation for this type of discipline. If I'm being honest, this type of discipline (or shall I say *nondiscipline*) is much harder than any discipline you have ever tried before. Why? Because it requires you to carefully consider a variety of factors and pillars instead of simply following a simple 1-2-3 process or doling out a specific punishment to fit the crime. It's hard, yes, but it will also pay big dividends as your child grows. A little hard work now for huge rewards later seems worth it, right?

Therefore, I want to spend a bit of time talking about what I consider to be the four pillars to this book: discipleship, not discipline; desire, not obedience; connection, not control; and growth, not assistance.

1. DISCIPLESHIP, NOT DISCIPLINE

Put on then, as God's chosen ones, holy and beloved, compassionate hearts, kindness, humility, meekness and patience, bearing with one another, and if one has a complaint against another, forgiving each other, as the Lord has forgiven you, so you also must forgive.

COLOSSIANS 3:12–13 (ESV)

I had just done the unthinkable: I told a woman to stop disciplining her son.

I was speaking at a Mothers of Preschoolers (MOPS) group and a young mom—we'll call her Susanna—raised her hand and told the story of her four-year-old son, James. James was really pushing his limits. He was running through her house, throwing balls at windows, smashing Lego towers built by his older brother, and then screaming when anyone told him to stop.

She told me she was at a loss.

That the time-outs and spankings and lectures she'd tried—tricks people had told her were sure to work—weren't working with her wild, strong-willed son.

That she didn't know where to turn.

That she was worried there was something wrong with her parenting and, worse, that there was something wrong with her son.

My heart broke for Susanna—and for the hundreds of other moms who have sat in my office with similar stories—but I also felt a glimmer of happiness as I heard her question. Because I know there is hope for kids like James.

And it starts when their parents stop disciplining them.

It's shocking, I know, but let me explain.

I am fully aware that if Susanna just stopped disciplining James, their entire household would crumble into a big, sticky, Lego-strewn mess. But I also know that the typical discipline strategies that all parents talk about just don't work for kids like James. Kids who know what they want and know how to get it. Kids who need Jesus, not a bunch of rules and boundaries.

Which is why our mind-set when it comes to discipline needs to change: Instead of disciplining them to behave, we have to disciple our kids' hearts to *want* to behave! Our kids don't need us to control them, to break their will, to punish crimes, or to teach them to obey. They need us to show their hearts what it means to follow Jesus wholeheartedly.

And that comes from adding a whole lot of discipleship into our discipline.

The truth is that our kids don't need to be fixed—which is what discipline often feels like. *Instead, they need to be understood and to be valued in the process of correction—which is what discipleship is all about.*

It means letting the Bible, rather than a surefire discipline method, guide our conversations with our kids. It means being nimble enough to give our kids justice, mercy, and grace when they need it. And it means stopping to consider our kids' hearts at every turn before jumping in and inflicting another consequence.

Discipleship is the key to our kids' hearts.

And it's the key to stopping misbehavior as well.

2. DESIRE, NOT OBEDIENCE

Delight yourself in the Lord, and he will give you the desires of your heart.

PSALM 37:4 (ESV)

The most—let's call them *passionate*—reactions that I've gotten to our book *Free to Parent* have been around the concept of replacing obedience with desire. And I get it. Parents have been conditioned for years to look at obedience as the ultimate sign that our kids are being raised right. Don't get me wrong, obedience *is* important. In the Bible, God calls each of us to obey his commandments in multiple verses (e.g., Romans 1:5 and Hebrews 13:17), and in Ephesians 6 children are instructed very clearly to obey their parents. Plus, practically speaking, how are our kids going to learn to obey teachers and bosses and even (gulp!) the law if they don't learn to obey their parents first?

I hear you, just as I've heard all of the other parents who have brought this same argument to me. But I stand by my original assertion: Obedience isn't the answer to this problem. Instead, the solution is to teach our kids to desire what's right.

My husband has a ninety-pound Labradoodle named Rufus. Please notice that I said my husband has a dog named Rufus. Rufus is not mine and has never been mine, and in fact, if it were up to me, Rufus would go live on a nice farm somewhere in Nova Scotia where he could chase little Canadian prairie dogs to his heart's content and stop squirming his way under my table to nip at my fingers while I eat. Suffice it to say, Rufus and I have a tempestuous relationship. Partly because he's big and drooly and can't keep his paws off my furniture, but mostly because he has an obedience issue: He has absolutely no desire to follow our house rules unless it results in a Milk-Bone.

Rufus has an excuse for this type of behavior: He is a dog.

You laugh, but in all honesty, I sometimes wonder if we are raising our kids as if they were Labradoodles. "Come here, kid! I'll give you a cookie if you obey me the first time!" While this sort of stick-and-carrot discipline can result in obedience—kids will do a lot to avoid punishment or gain a reward—I believe it does little to teach our kids to truly obey God in their hearts.

I think we need to rethink our definition of obedience. If our kids only obey us in order to avoid a consequence or to gain a reward, then are they really obeying? I don't think so. Instead, our goal as parents has to be to teach our kids to genuinely desire what is good, true, and beautiful; what is right, honest, and virtuous; what is godly and kind.

The truth is, obedience is simply not enough. When our end goal is to help our kids truly desire God, concepts like "first-time obedience" and even "consistent consequences" start to fall flat. These concepts—while useful as parenting tools—can teach our kids to have head knowledge of what is right and what is wrong. But going far beyond that, our kids need to learn how to direct the desires of their heart on a foundation of connected faith so they will understand how to truly desire what is good and right and beautiful and then reject what is evil.

There is a catch: Desire is much, much harder to teach our kids than simple obedience. Even Rufus can learn to obey—when he wants a treat. But teaching our kids to desire what is right is a lifelong process, one that will certainly be fraught with ups and downs, with failures and victories. But it is worth it: Because instead of teaching your kids to follow rules, you'll be giving them a glimpse into what it means to *seek* God with their entire hearts.

3. CONNECTION, NOT CONTROL

> *But I will instruct you and teach you in the way you should go; I will counsel you with my eye upon you. Be not like a horse or a mule, without understanding, which must be curbed with bit and bridle, or it will not stay near you.*
>
> PSALM 32: 8–9 (ESV)

It's so easy to try to control our kids.

Notice I didn't say it's so easy to control our kids—that's downright impossible—but it's really easy to fall into the trap of trying to control our kids' thoughts, emotions, and behaviors so they can turn out exactly how we want them to turn out.

I know I did that with my oldest daughter.

I grew up in a very difficult family—a place where control and fear seemed to rule us and where a heart connection was hard to be found. I remember when I won a spot at the district track meet in the ninth grade. I desperately wanted my dad—who had never attended a single one of my school events—to come see me run. I brought home the flyer for the district meet and presented it to him one night at dinner.

"Dad, would you like to come to my district track meet?" I held up the flyer, staring at my dad's eyes, hoping he would see my desperation, my heart. "I'll be running the 880."

"Ellen." His voice was gruff. "I just don't have time. But

maybe if you are really helpful around the house and behave well I'll be able to find the time."

I smiled. I could be helpful. I could behave. And so I set about to do the best I could. For two weeks, I volunteered to do dishes and to watch over my brothers and sisters. I filed paperwork for my dad at his office and did all of my homework without being asked. I was polite and kind and behaved the best I could.

Yet on the day of the meet, my dad didn't show up.

I was heartbroken.

Fast-forward twenty years to when I had my own kids who had their own sports events and recitals and art shows. From day one, I made it my vow to never let my kids feel the way I did at that track meet. I was going to attend every single event they ever had. I was going to cheer them on no matter what they did. I was going to be involved in their every move. I was going to give them every opportunity. I was never going to let fear of disappointment rule them.

I was going to... control their every emotion.

I learned this when my own oldest daughter was in middle school. She had a track meet on the same day as her sister's swim meet and I was desperately trying to figure out how I could drive across town in seven minutes flat so I could watch Alisa's hundred-meter butterfly without missing Erin's relay. And Erin stopped me.

"Mom, it's fine. You can watch Alisa today and watch me next time."

"But then you'll think I don't care and that I don't want to be part of your track career and that I care more about Alisa than you..." I'm sure I sounded desperate.

"We'll talk about it later, Mom. I know you care. I can tell by what you do every day."

And there it was. I can't control my kids' schedules or out-comes. I can't control my kids' behavior or thoughts. I can't control whether they finish their homework or chores or whether they love gymnastics or music or football. But I can be there for them. And connect with them on a deep level that shows that I care about them in a way that goes beyond simply knowing what they do.

Because I can know their hearts.

4. GROWTH, NOT ASSISTANCE

For this very reason, make every effort to supplement your faith with virtue, and virtue with knowledge, and knowledge with self-control, and self-control with steadfastness, and steadfastness with godliness, and godliness with brotherly affection, and broth-erly affection with love. For if these qualities are yours and are increasing, they keep you from being ineffective or unfruitful in the knowledge of our Lord Jesus Christ.

2 PETER 1: 5–8 (ESV)

I probably don't have to remind you, but you are an adult. You have already navigated the lessons of childhood and you have moved on to adulthood. You know how to manage your money. You have learned about things like respect and friendship and compassion and empathy. You have passed the fifth grade.

And that means that even if your kid is asking you for the tenth time for twenty dollars for gas to fill up his car because he spent his last dollar on chewing gum, or telling you how every girl in the entire grade is being mean to her, you can't solve these problems for your kids. They have to figure it out for themselves.

Which is why as you read this book, you'll find that we often encourage parents to let their kids solve their own problems, to come up with their own consequences, to work through their own issues. This isn't because we're being mean or lazy or because we don't want to fork over twenty dollars, but simply because we know that kids learn more when they are forced to grow.

PUTTING THE FOUR PILLARS INTO ACTION

I realize this chapter is very pie-in-the-sky—that I've just introduced some major, heart-changing ideas and then given you very little practical advice to help you understand how to implement them in your life. And whether you're saying, "Okay, I'm going to try this" or "I'm not so sure yet," I have a feeling that you are a bit confused on what to do next. And how to make this work for your family.

Don't worry.

We're going to get there. For now, I wanted to give you a big picture overview of what we're going to be talking about as we share real discipline stories with real parents in the coming chapters. In the rest of this book, you'll find real-life practical tips on how to put these concepts into action as well as ideas on how these pillars can help you to connect to your kids in a meaningful way.

So if you're feeling confused, overwhelmed, unsure, or anything else right now, hang with us.

PUT THE
DISCIPLE
INTO
DISCIPLINE

CHAPTER 1

Six Quick Tips to Get the Most Out of This Book

WE'RE ALMOST TO THE GOOD PART. We promise!

But before we dive in, we wanted to give you a quick guide that you can reference as you read to make sure you get the most out of this book.

TIP #1: READ THE WHOLE BOOK THROUGH EVEN IF YOU THINK A PARTICULAR SCENARIO DOESN'T APPLY TO YOU

If there is one thing I (Erin) have learned from those times when my kids are embarrassingly, awkwardly, and mortifyingly misbehaving, it's this: You never know what parenting is going to throw at you. I never expected my (usually) sweet nine-year-old girl to get into a fists-out brawl with her little brother over a dog toy. I never expected to get a call from the school that my child had stood on his chair and danced during class. And I never expected my first grader to come home from school using the F-word. I used to think that I was exempt from these sorts of things because, well, I'm a good

Christian mom who takes my kids to church every Sunday and feeds them organic carrots for lunch. I should be off the hook, right?

Wrong.

Big parenting issues happen in all of our kids' lives, at different times and in different places, but they happen to all of us. So we chose scenarios for this book that we believe most parents will stumble across at one point or another in their parenting years. Whether you have toddlers or teenagers, we believe that many of the concepts woven into these scenarios are universal. Kids of all ages can be strong-willed, jealous, angry, impulsive, mean, dishonest, and disrespectful. Kids of all ages can also understand big concepts like redemption, love, kindness, honesty, loyalty, respect, and forgiveness. And so while a particular scenario may not hit you at your current parenting stage, we do believe that it could include a few of the tools you need to truly connect with your kids.

TIP #2: TRY NOT TO JUDGE

It is very easy to judge other parents.

I think we all do it. I (Erin) remember attending a dance class with my daughter and watching as another child consistently interrupted the teacher. She was off doing her own pirouettes when the other kids (my daughter included) were doing toe touches. When the kids were doing pirouettes, this girl was doing somersaults. I remember grumbling to myself that that girl's parents should probably keep better tabs on their daughter and that they needed to show her some discipline.

Then, last week, I got a dose of my own medicine. I was at a gymnastics class and another mom came up to me and said, "Your son is disrupting the class for the other kids. Maybe you need to find a way to get him under control." I walked onto the gym floor and sure enough, my son was being a total pain. I pulled him out of the class and had him watch until he decided he could listen to the teacher. That said, I felt a bit irritated at the other mom for chastising me. How could she know what I have done to discipline my son? Who is she to say I'm not "finding a way to keep him under control"? Who is she to judge my parenting?

Then I remembered the dance class.

I had done the exact same thing. Okay, I hadn't told the other mom what to do, but I had thought about it. There's a real temptation to think, "That kid is really messing up" or "My kid would never do that" or even "That kid is ruining this for all the other kids." That may or may not be true, but we have to remember something else: We haven't walked in another parent's shoes. We don't know what's going on in another kid's life. And we certainly don't know how God is working in another kid's heart.

So, as you read this, we encourage you to learn, to pray, and to think but not to judge. Sure, your son may never look up hot cheerleaders kissing football players on the iPad. (More on that in the next chapter—it's a doozy!) And your daughter may never run crazy in dance class, ignoring what the teacher has to say. But every kid has something—some place in their heart— where God has work to do. Whether your kid's rough spots are obvious or hidden, they are there. And so I ask you to read with a heart that loves Jesus and wants the best for each of his kids.

TIP #3: PAY ATTENTION TO THE MAJOR THEMES

If your kid looks up "hot girls" on the iPad, it's about a whole lot more than a simple iPad search. And if your kid lies about brushing her teeth, it's about a whole lot more than a hygiene issue. Every little behavior your child exhibits has undercurrents that mean a whole lot more. As you read these scenarios, we want you to pay special attention to the bigger themes that come out of each situation.

To make this easy, we've put the key words in boxes in each section. As you have conversations with your kids, we encourage you to look for undercurrents of these major themes in the words your kids say and consider how they are affecting your kids' behavior. This will help you to know where and how your kid is struggling and how to springboard conversation.

TIP #4: USE THE THEMES AS FUTURE TALKING POINTS

I have had many, many great conversations with my son in the weeks that followed the hot cheerleader incident. We've talked about marriage and purity and kissing and relationships and even the media's influence on our culture. As you read these scenarios—especially the ones that hit close to home with your own kids—I encourage you to use those major themes as jumping-off points for future conversations.

So, for example, if you face a situation where your child lies to you, deal with that conversation in the moment. But in the weeks following the incident, consider telling him a story about a time you lied as a child. Or talk about a person in your life who has been honest and how you can trust him. You can even talk about things like politics and scandal and trust. As you have these conversations, you don't have to bring up the major issues from before; instead, use them as tools to spark deeper understanding and connection with your kids.

TIP #5: SHARE THIS BOOK WITH YOUR SPOUSE

We're preaching to the choir when we tell you that effective discipleship will come when you and your spouse approach your kids as a united front. Share this with your husband or wife. Let them know that this is what you are trying and allow them to share in the joy of discipleship and connection.

TIP #6: PRAY OFTEN AND INTENTIONALLY

Again, we're telling you things that you surely already know, but in order for you to effectively and lovingly disciple your kids, you have to allow yourself to be led by the One who knows your kids' hearts best.

I (Ellen) have kept a prayer journal for more than twenty years now. In it, I record my daily prayers, as well as the many ways God has answered those prayers. These journals have served as encouragement for my kids (and for me!), as I can go back through them and see the many powerful ways God moves through prayer.

As you start this discipleship process, we ask you to commit to pray for your kids' hearts on a daily basis. Pray specifically for the areas that you hope to disciple in them and ask God for answers and for true conversation that will lead them toward Him. If you can, record these prayers so you can go back and see how God has moved, and watch as miracles unfold.

CHAPTER 2

The Hot Cheerleader Incident

(ERIN)

Hot cheerleaders kissing football players.

The five words glaring up at me from my iPad search engine bar felt like a punch in the gut.

I read them again.

A lump rose in my throat and my mind began to race. My ten-year-old son and his friend Braden had been playing what I assumed was Minecraft on the iPad in the living room while I made dinner. And though I hadn't been paying the best attention, I had assumed that everything was fine. They were ten years old, for goodness' sake. How much trouble could they get into on an iPad?

I had clearly assumed wrong.

I did what any mom would do at that moment: I started to cry. Then my mind began to race. Obviously, my son was grounded from technology, chocolate, and fun until he was twenty-six. And the iPad would clearly need to go into the trash. And I would never be able to trust my son around any screened device again for as long as he lived in my house. And...

I stopped myself.

Because while my gut instinct as a mom was to get angry and start doling out punishment, my heart screamed at me that there had to be another way. A way of grace and truth and love and hope. A way where my relationship with my son wouldn't be sacrificed even when his behavior needed to be dealt with in a serious way.

So I called my mom.

Now, before I go any further, I have to tell you a little bit about my mom. She's awesome. And not just your everyday awesome, but she has worked with kids for more than forty years, as an educator, a mom, and a grandma. Because of this, she seems to innately know how our words can help our kids to truly grow closer to God. She has said for years that discipline is so much more than obedience and control and lectures and punishment. Instead, she tells parents that only by replacing obedience with a desire for what is right, control with a heartfelt connection, lectures with truth spoken in love, and so-called discipline with discipleship can parents truly raise kids who love God and others in a heartfelt way.

That's a tall order and something that every parent struggles with. But as I've implemented these principles, I have found that my parenting has changed. And, more importantly, my kids' hearts have changed.

Anyway, back to hot cheerleaders kissing football players.

I told my mom what I had found on my iPad. Part of me expected her to be ashamed or to lecture me about how I had to tighten up my screen controls, but instead she said, "This is good, Erin."

"Good? How can this be good? My ten-year-old and his friends are searching for videos of hot cheerleaders on YouTube."

"I know, Erin, and we'll need to deal with this. But isn't it good that this happened now? Because now you have an opportunity to truly speak to his heart, to walk through this with him when his mind is still innocent and his heart is still willing. In our world, he's going to stumble across things like this, and whether he's ten or twenty-nine, it will affect him. Isn't it good that it happened now when the stakes are still low? When you can still guide him through it?"

She was right. I knew it. But how was I going to guide my son through something like...that?

I stared at those five words on my screen, and a stream of big, adult words with real-world consequences flooded through my mind. Words like *pornography, sex, purity, gender roles, addiction, respect*, and *lust*. How do you talk to a ten-year-old about big adult concepts like these when they've hardly begun to scrape the surface of knowing about the birds and the bees?

My mom gave me some ideas. Then she prayed with me.

And I began the long trek up the stairs.

"Joey? Can I come in?" He was sitting at his desk working on homework. He saw the iPad in my hands and his eyebrows rose. "I...uh...found something on the iPad that really worries me."

His eyes widened and he got up and plopped onto his bed. "I know, Mom."

"You do?"

He turned to me, wide-eyed, and his words gushed out. "Braden and I were watching YouTube videos of football players and then there was this video of cheerleaders and then we remembered some of the older kids at school were saying that the cheerleaders were hot and..." His voice trailed off and I bit my lip, resisting the urge to lecture, to punish.

"And what?"

"And I don't know, Mom. I mean, it can't be bad to watch football players play football because Daddy does it with me all the time. And it can't be bad to watch cheerleaders cheer because they always cheer at football games. So when I saw that video, I figured it couldn't be bad to watch it because it's just football players and cheerleaders...." His words drifted off again, and I could tell he wasn't sure what to say. So I waited.

"But, Mom..." he started again, his voice choked. "I felt a little sick when I was watching it. I don't know why but it didn't feel right."

And there it was: the perfect opportunity for me to disciple my son.

I grabbed his hand and led him downstairs where I made cocoa. We sat on the couch and talked for more than an hour about all of those big words that felt so beyond his scope of understanding just hours ago.

We talked about how watching videos of football players isn't necessarily bad and watching videos of cheerleaders isn't necessarily bad. But when the words *hot* and *kissing* entered the equation, a whole lot of disrespect entered the equation. We talked about honoring girls by not labeling them as hot. We talked about how things like kissing are private and not something others should be watching. We even talked about how videos like the one he saw—which was fairly innocent as far as such videos go—often lead to much more graphic videos. I even told him the basics of how Internet pornography works—how a computer can record the videos you see and then suggest others that can eventually lead you down a path that you never wanted to go. We talked about lust and marriage and God's design for sex. The whole time I was silently praying that God would speak through me, letting my words take root in the heart of my precious son.

Joey just listened. He asked a few questions. We prayed. And he went to bed.

But the next morning, he walked downstairs with an announcement. "Mom, I've decided that I'm never using a computer or iPad again. It's just not worth the risk." I had to chuckle—that had been my initial thought when I saw that he had watched the video too.

"That's not logical, Joey. Computers and iPads are an important part of our lives. I use mine to work. I write stories, check my e-mail, test apps."

He looked at me wide-eyed. "So how can I make sure that I never see a video like that again? You told me that the iPad has recorded that I watched it and it might...um, it might... show me another one."

"Great question, Joey. That's why we have to put safeguards on screens and the use of devices. To protect you from things like that. What do you think we can do to protect you?"

He thought about it for a minute and then looked up at me. "I know! We can require that when I'm using the iPad, someone else has to be sitting with me—like an adult."

"Would that make you feel more safe?"

"Yes, I think I'd like that."

I had to walk out of the room at that point and do a little fist pump. My son had inflicted a punishment on himself that was the exact same punishment I would have doled out the night before: no screen time unless an adult is with you. Only he did it to himself. Willingly. Because he wanted to do it. Same end result, only now he was feeling a true desire to do right, instead of a whole bunch of anger at his mean old mom and dad.

This conversation and the many productive, heartfelt conversations I had with my son in the weeks to follow have led me to ask the question that I have wondered about for so long: What if we are getting discipline wrong as parents?

What if a God-honoring, obedient heart doesn't come from

a bunch of strict rules, clearly defined consequences, and stern punishments? What if there's more to parenting than following a "good parent" formula, than saying the right things, than having the right rules? What if in order for our kids to truly connect with God, they must first truly connect with us, in a loving, honest, open, and heartfelt way?

Those are the questions we are asking in this book.

We want to take you through those tough parenting moments—those "hot cheerleaders kissing football players" incidents where you feel your heart drop and you have no idea what to say. Because at those moments, you have a choice to make: Are you going to choose discipline, or are you going to choose discipleship?

We hope it's the latter.

And we hope this book will help you get there.

CHAPTER 3

The Fruit of the Spirit Is . . . Self-Control

(ERIN)

A man without self-control is like a city broken into and left with-out walls.

PROVERBS 25:28 (ESV)

I PEEKED OUT THE DOOR while I was making dinner a few weeks ago and saw five-year-old Will standing on top of the swing set. He stood there proudly, holding a stick in one hand and a watering can in the other, his chest puffed out, seemingly unaware that he was ten feet above the ground and if he fell, well, I didn't even want to think about it.

My first instinct was to race out the door yelling at him to climb down, but I realized that quick movements could make him fall—or do something impulsive like jump. So I took a deep breath and forced a smile. "Hey, buddy, looks like you are really high. I'm worried that's not safe. Can you please come down?"

"Hi, Mama! Don't worry! I'm holding your watering can really tight."

Oh, perfect! As long as you don't drop my three-year-old plastic watering can, then we're all good! Carry on! I mean, seriously, child?

I crept over to him and held up my hands. "Will, it's very

important that you get down right now. I want you to drop the stick and the watering can, then carefully sit and climb down the side right here where Mommy is."

He shrugged, sat down, swung forward onto the swing set pole like it was a bar, and adeptly dropped into my waiting arms. No harm, no foul.

I took a deep breath and quickly prayed for wisdom. And the sanity not to call my husband and demand that he take the swing set apart that very instant.

"Will, what were you thinking when you climbed up to the top of the swing set? That's very dangerous and you could have gotten hurt."

He smiled toothily. "I just wanted to be a pirate on the top of my ship. I was the lookout pirate. I could see the entire sea from up there."

Mmm-hmm. The entire sea.

I wanted to scream and rant and put him in time-out for a year, but the truth is, I saw his point. He wasn't trying to be dangerous or disobedient; he was just lost in his own imaginary world. And when he saw the lookout tower, he went. Without even considering the consequences. Or considering how he could, say, demonstrate self-control.

In my work with parents (not to mention my text messages from my friends), I'm starting to find that so many kids lack self-control. These are not necessarily naughty or disobedient kids—although they can certainly seem like it—but rather are kids who need to learn how to control those crazy, climb-to-the-top-of-the-swing-set impulses.

I've learned that these types of kids need specific types of discipleship. That was true for my son, and I've seen it even more as I've received letters like the one from Susanna below:

Dear Erin,

My four-year-old son James has pushed me to the limit. He is systematically destroying our house, our peace, our schedule, and our family dynamics. He runs through our house uncontrolled, jumping on couches, throwing balls at windows, smashing the Lego towers built by his older brother, and then screaming when we ask him to stop.

I am at a loss. He is our third child, and his two older siblings never acted like this. Before I had James, I thought I knew all of the parenting "tricks" and was confident I knew how to raise a healthy, obedient child. But I'm learning that I was wrong. Because no matter what I try with James—time-outs, spankings, lectures, loss of privileges— he seems bent on doing the same destructive things over and over.

Honestly, I'm terrified to send him to school next year. I imagine teachers wouldn't look very kindly on a child who jumps on tables, throws school supplies across the room, and then screams when asked to stop. I'm embarrassed! And not sure where to turn. Do you have any ideas?

Help!
Susanna

If there is anyone I can relate to, it's a parent who is trying to help her son or daughter find self-control. After all, I have definitely been there, done that with my son Will. And my other kids at times. So whenever a mom writes to me with these types of questions, the first thing I want to do is pull her over for a big hug, then reassure her that really, truly, pinky-promise, it will be okay.

Dear Susanna,

I think your son James and my youngest son Will would be great friends. Of course, I'm not sure the world would ever be the same with the trouble they could cause!

We (somewhat affectionately) call Will "the Path" which is short for "Path of Destruction" because he can literally tear through our house leaving a path of tears, screaming, and chaos behind him before I am even able to register what is happening. A few weeks ago, I heard some banging upstairs. I raced up to find a pile of what was previously folded laundry strewn along the stairs. I followed the path of laundry to Will's room, where the laundry basket was tipped over by his closet. He had used it to climb up the shelving in his closet, hang from the closet bar, and swing himself onto the top shelf, where he was happily lying reading a book.

I honestly believe that kids like James and Will aren't inherently mean or destructive or even disobedient at heart. I think they are simply kids who have a hard time controlling their impulses. If it looks like fun to leap onto the table, to knock over a Lego tower, or to swing from their closet bar, they do it—without thinking about the consequences of how it will affect others. And when we as parents dole out punishment for their antics, we may be teaching them not to jump onto their sister's tea party, but we aren't teaching them to consider the implications of their actions before they do something.

I'm certainly not there with Will—I caught him drinking out of the toilet with a silly straw just yesterday—but we're getting there. And I have a few ideas about what you can do to help James while keeping your sanity—and your house—intact.

Erin

BIG-PICTURE THEMES

- Obedience
- Kindness
- Self-control
- Empathy
- Listening to adults

- Following rules
- Respect
- Taking care of property
- Living together with others in harmony

DISCIPLESHIP FOR THE CHILD WHO LACKS SELF-CONTROL

> *Every athlete exercises self-control in all things. They do it to receive a perishable wreath, but we an imperishable.*
>
> I CORINTHIANS 9:25 (ESV)

It's easy to live in the moment with kids—especially kids who are bent on causing destruction. With Will, we found that our tendency was to spend a lot of time talking about situations where he lacked self-control but less time showing him examples of how he could develop it. Interestingly, it was when we started talking about the virtue of self-control outside of the context of his own misbehavior that he started really internalizing it. And wanting to change it.

But with a child who lacks self-control, our work is twofold: We have to help them to stop impulsivity and gain control, and we have to show them what having self-control looks like. The next section of this book is full of tips for stopping impulsivity when it happens (i.e., the discipline), but before that, we encourage you to set a vision for your child about what Jesus means when He asks us to be self-controlled (i.e., the discipleship). Here are a few ideas:

- **Talk about what self-control means.** In the verse at the beginning of this section, 1 Corinthians 9:25, we learn that every athlete exercises self-control in all things. Its important to look at the context of the word *athlete*—in other versions, that word is translated as "a man striving for mastery" (KJV) or "one who competes" (NIV). I tell Will it means "anyone who wants to do something and do it well." The verse goes on to say that this athlete exercises self-control in all things so he can find success. We talk about how when we find ways to show self-control, we set ourselves up to be exactly the person God made us to be, and in doing so, help earn an "imperishable wreath."

- **Read Bible stories or children's books that focus on self-control.** Tell your kids about the life of Peter, who grew from an impulsive follower of Christ to a steadfast pillar of the church. How David refused to harm Saul in 1 Samuel 24. How Daniel and his friends purposed to not eat the king's food in Daniel 1. How Jesus was steadfast when He was tempted by Satan in the wilderness in Matthew 4.

- **Help your kid to focus on who he is rather than what he does.** That way, he can rise up and become the person God created him to be. Try phrases like:

  - I am a child of the One True King.
  - I was created to glorify Him all the days of my life.
  - I have been given the ability to show self-control from the Creator of the world.

- **Tell stories about kids who do have self-control.** "My friend Sarah told me about a child who found a candy bar at the park. The child wanted to eat it, but he realized that would be wrong. It could be stealing from someone who accidentally left it there, not to mention it could have made him sick."

- **Help your child to memorize a Bible verse about self-control.** Some that I like are:

  o "Whoever guards his mouth preserves his life; he who opens wide his lips comes to ruin" (Proverbs 13:3 ESV).

  o "A man without self-control is like a city broken into and left without walls" (Proverbs 25:28 ESV).

  o "Good sense makes one slow to anger, and it is his glory to overlook an offense" (Proverbs 19:11 ESV).

  o "Look carefully then how you walk, not as unwise but as wise, making the best use of the time, because the days are evil" (Ephesians 5:15–16 ESV).

- **Hang up a character board in your home.** Work with your child to draw pictures of things that demonstrate self-control, such as a kid who is careful with someone else's toy or a kid who is kind to a friend. Or, if your child is old enough to write, have them copy verses or sayings about self-control. Hang them in an area of your home that your child sees often and add to the board whenever you can.

PRACTICAL SOLUTIONS FOR A CHILD WHO LACKS SELF-CONTROL

For wisdom will come into your heart, and knowledge will be pleasant to your soul; discretion will watch over you, understanding will guard you.

PROVERBS 2:10–11 (ESV)

I'm learning this is the mode of operation with kids like Will and James. They are highly creative, highly curious, and highly ambitious—and they haven't quite developed the self-control to temper those qualities in order to stay safe and out of trouble. The outcome of this is that these kids are labeled as behavior problems—kids who don't listen to instruction, don't obey, don't follow directions, and, perhaps worst of all, kids who are aggressive and hyperactive. When these kids get to school, they are often shifted from classroom to classroom, labeled as inattentive and unable to learn, when the reality is that they simply need to learn to stop and think.

I don't want my baby to be labeled as a behavior problem! There are, of course, times when every child is defiant and disobedient, but I think often kids who lack self-control are simply unable to process their thoughts in a way that leads to order. And that's something that can be changed. Here are a few ideas:

1. Ask for a Redo
Pillar: Growth

My Will can cause a lot of damage in just a few minutes. A few months ago, I asked him to go upstairs and get a pair of socks and then come back down to put on his shoes. I waited five minutes and when Will hadn't come down, I headed up the stairs to investigate. I found him in his brother Joey's room with a pile of football cards on the floor. Football cards that Joey had carefully arranged in binders the day before.

I was furious.

And I couldn't even begin to imagine what his brother would think.

While I knew Will would certainly have to go back and help Joey clean up the cards, I wanted to get right back to the point of impulsivity. So I told him to do a redo. Together we walked back down the stairs. I had him stand in the exact same spot he had stood five minutes before when I had asked him to go upstairs, and I told him once again to head up and grab a pair of socks. Then I had him go up the stairs again and instead of stopping by Joey's door—the moment he lost his self-control—go into his own room and get his socks.

Then we talked about the moment he lost self-control and how he could have avoided it.

He did later have to work with Joey to help him reorganize his football cards—a natural consequence. The immediate consequence to redo the moment when he lost self-control was a way to show him how to overcome the impulse he felt and do the right thing. Here are a few ways to try:

- "Wow! What a mess. Our family's rule is that we empty our backpacks at the kitchen table and then hang them on the hooks. Why don't you pick up the bags from the floor, head back outside, and come inside again and put them away correctly."
- "It's never kind to hit even if you are angry. Why don't you head back over to your brother and show me how you could respond to your frustrations in a way that honors God."
- "I can tell you didn't think before you threw that shovelful of rocks on the playground. Why don't you go apologize to the kids who were sitting nearby and then show me how you can use your shovel to fill up that bucket."

- "Whoa! When you talk to me like that, it makes me wonder if you are considering your words before you speak. Why don't you close your eyes and count to ten and then tell me what you really meant to say."

These phrases give kids a chance to go back to the moment when they made the wrong decision and reconsider their actions. It teaches them to consider their impulses and gives them an opportunity to right what is wrong.

2. Be Patient with Consequences
Pillar: Desire

A child who lacks self-control needs to learn to pause and consider implications in the moment. And while a consequence helps them to remember past implications, it does little to teach them to pause in the moment. In the story above, had I immediately made Will clean up the cards, he would have learned not to mess with his brother's things but wouldn't have learned how to consider implications when he is in the moment. You can help your child to desire to do right—even when they have an impulse to do wrong—simply by teaching them to consider their own thought processes. Try:

- "Can you tell me what you were thinking about right before you pushed your sister?"
- "That was a silly thing to do. Can you tell me what made you decide to do it?"
- "It's clear that you didn't pause to think before you acted there. What were you thinking about instead?"
- "Let's talk about what was going through your head at school today so we can come up with some strategies to help you have self-control in class."

- "I wonder if saying a quick prayer before
  thing would help you to have more self-c

3. Explain Your Own Thought Processes
Pillar: Connection

I threw a dirty towel at my husband last night. I'm not talking about tossing it to him underhanded while asking him to
throw it in the laundry. No, I bunched it up into a ball and
chucked it at him as hard as I could. Now you know where
Will gets it.

My excuse was simple: I was frustrated. Cameron had
walked in after work and set his bag down on the kitchen
table—the table I was just getting ready to set. Then he had
disappeared into his room to change while I tried to juggle
three hungry kids and a dinner that was burning. So, when
he walked out of the room all nonchalantly, I lost it. I threw the
towel at him.

If we're being honest, we all have a bit of trouble controlling our impulses from time to time. Even as responsible,
mature adults. One of the best ways we can teach our kids to
control their impulses is to show them how we learn to control
our own. Try saying things like:

- "That was pretty silly when I threw that towel at Daddy.
  I was feeling really frustrated and I acted without thinking. What I should have done was to take a deep breath
  and tell Daddy to please move his bag off the table."
- "Oh, wow. I just knocked over that entire basket of laundry when I wasn't looking. I should probably remember
  to put that up on the bed next time."
- "I'm sorry I yelled at you. I was really angry that you
  chose not to listen to me, but we both know that me

doing the wrong thing certainly didn't help. Can you forgive me? Next time I am going to work to stay calm even when I am angry."

- "One time when I was a little girl, I snuck into my sister's room and played with her favorite tea set when she wasn't home. I accidentally broke the handle! I felt terrible and from then on, I remembered how important it was to respect other people's property."

4. Consider Sensory Issues
Pillar: Growth

I need to be very clear that I am not a doctor or a therapist and thus cannot speak intelligently about disorders like sensory integration. I also need to be clear that if you suspect your child is struggling with sensory integration disorder, you need to seek professional help right away.

That said, I think a lot of kids—especially young kids—have trouble figuring out the sensory input they receive each day. They may hear things more loudly than others, feel things more intensely than others, or see things differently than others. Because of this, they may struggle with impulse control, especially when they are feeling sensations that may be different from their norm.

My son Will falls into this category, and while my doctor has evaluated him and doesn't feel like he has a sensory processing disorder, she did recommend that we take a few steps to help him better understand the sensory input that he gets every day. She told us that all kids—even those without a diagnosis—can benefit from a change in sensory input at certain times. By changing up the sensations they are feeling, kids often find themselves better able to consider their behavior and have better self-control. Try:

- When your kid is seeming to lack self-control, try pulling him into a tight hug or sitting and snuggling on the couch under a blanket.
- If your kid is struggling to calm down or sleep at night, purchase a weighted blanket—I got mine for seventy dollars on Etsy. This helps some kids relax and settle down.
- Turn down the lights, or if it's a dark and dreary day, turn on all the lamps.
- Try a quick foot or hand massage. Use aromatic lotion or an essential oil that claims to be "calming" or "relaxing."
- Turn on some calming music. Or if your child is acting morose, turn on dance music and dance with her.
- Make hot tea or cocoa and drink it with your child.
- Change the scenery. Go for a drive, go outside, go into a different room. Do something to change where they are at so their behavior has to change as well.

GAINING SELF-CONTROL

With young, inquisitive, curious, and, yes, impulsive kids like James and Will, self-control is one of the hardest things to teach. These kids try—they really do—but as pirate ships merge with Play-Doh, they just lose any ability to have self-control. It's who they are and who God made them.

The truth is, we've all felt that way at times. For every one of us, there are those moments when we get carried away by emotions, by situations, by excitement and just...lose it. So have empathy for your child. Tell them you understand. And then give them the tools they need to overcome their impulsivity and to show the world the person God wants them to be:

Joyful yet controlled.
Creative yet measured.
Obedient yet full of life.

———

Dear Jesus,

I want to lift up Susanna and James and all of the other parents who have kids who seem to carve a path of destruction through life. God, I pray that You fill these sweet children with a desire to do right and these loving parents with the patience they need to walk their kids through their younger years so they become loving, kind, and self-controlled adults. Give their parents a unique discernment that allows them to know the exact words to say and actions to take to guide their children's hearts toward you.

Amen

—— CHAPTER 4 ——

Perfect Love Is Better Than Perfection
(ELLEN)

There is no fear in love, but perfect love casts out fear. For fear has to do with punishment, and whoever fears has not been perfected in love.

1 JOHN 4:18 (ESV)

MY YOUNGEST DAUGHTER, ALISA, gave early indications that she was a perfectionist. She grew frustrated and crumpled her artwork each time it did not look just right. Even as a young girl, she would ask, "Is it possible to be perfect?" and listen attentively for my response. She certainly was not the stereotypical youngest child, competing fiercely even with her older siblings. With her own peers, only the highest outcomes were acceptable in everything she set out to do.

Alisa's response to her perfectionism was to overachieve. She battled to be the best at everything, often spending hours doing her homework to make sure it was just right. If she couldn't do a cartwheel, she would go into the yard and practice. And practice and practice and practice and practice until she figured it out. In time, however, we began to see signs of deep-seated anxiety. As soon as she reached one goal, her joy was short lived, as she would soon begin to drive herself to still a higher goal. Failure to Alisa was getting second place at the state swim meet or failing to break a state record in her best events or not getting the highest score on a math exam. She authentically felt like a failure when she did not reach the very highest marks she set for herself.

I know I probably sound like one of those mothers who does that weird pseudo-complaining thing. "Woe is me! My kid always did her homework on the first try and it made it so hard for us to have a social life." And I get it: We were very fortunate. But Alisa's driven perfectionism also caused some problems, mainly that she based her worth entirely on whether she accomplished what she set out to do. Alisa likely would have achieved even more with a healthy outlook.

Yes, you read that right. I believe that perfectionist kids could be higher achievers if they were able to deal with their perfectionism. The flip side is that some perfectionists, like the girl Carrie described in the letter below, respond to their perfectionism by underachieving. Either way, perfectionists stand in the way of their own success.

Dear Ellen,

Help! I'm going crazy. My daughter Carrie (age 8) comes home from school every day and insists that she just wants to rest and hang out. When I ask about homework, my question is met with a combination of tears and outright refusal. It seems like she would rather fail the third grade than spend twenty minutes doing her math.

Yesterday, I reached a breaking point. I asked Carrie to get out her math assignment and she immediately stormed up the stairs and threw herself onto her bed. I followed her and sat down, only to be barraged with "I can't do math; I'm too stupid," and "Math is too hard for me right now; I'm not going to do it." I told her she had no choice and threatened that she would lose her play date this weekend if she didn't finish her math, and finally she came downstairs. But even with her worksheet in front of her she just stared at the problems, refusing to even try to get the right answers. Two hours later, we had three of the fifteen problems done.

I'm not sure if I can do this! Spending two hours doing math problems is not my idea of a fun Tuesday night, not to mention the fact that it breaks my heart to hear my daughter tell me she is "too stupid" or math is "too hard"—especially considering that she's never had trouble with math before. Anyway, what can I do to stop these homework battles?

Sincerely,

Joe

From Joe's description, I can see that Carrie has a drive to succeed—to do things well and to do them right—but because that seems impossible, she has instead given up. Her response is to set low aims—no homework done or no play to audition for or no sports team to make. The risk of not reaching her goals is too terrifying even to try. Here's how I responded to Joe:

Dear Joe,

My first word of encouragement: You are not alone!

I have parents come into my office nearly on a daily basis describing a very similar problem to this one. And, regardless of the kids' age, performance, and gifting, I'm finding that more times than not, homework battles are a result of perfectionism.

I know that actually could sound funny to you—I'm calling a kid a perfectionist who you think is going to fail the third grade. But hear me out. Kids who are perfectionists usually respond to their innate desire to be flawless and without fault in one of two ways: Either they overachieve, which often results in deep-seated anxiety and profound discouragement as their goals remain out of reach, or they underachieve, putting on an "I don't care" or an "I can't do it anyway" mask to cover up their feelings of helplessness and their fear of failure.

Both reactions can result in a lot of stress for both the parent and the kid—and both reactions can result in a lot of anxiety and struggle around homework time. It sounds to me like Carrie is a perfectionist—her refusal to work and her crying out that she's "too stupid" to finish the work, even when she has never struggled before and has no documented learning disabilities, tells me that there is something in her that is scared to try, because she is scared to fail. While it seems daunting to deal with it, I know some tricks and conversations to help you and her get over the hump.

Sincerely,
Ellen

BIG PICTURE THEMES

- Perfectionism
- Hard work
- Stress

- Laziness
- Effort
- Talents and spiritual gifts

DISCIPLESHIP FOR A CHILD WHO IS A PERFECTIONIST

But he said to me, "My grace is sufficient for you, for my power is made perfect in weakness."

2 CORINTHIANS 12:9 (ESV)

I have dozens of parents who arrange coaching sessions with me every year to talk about their perfectionist children. But when they set up the initial conversation, they almost never tell me they have a perfectionist on their hands. Instead, they say things like:

- "My son is lazy. He never gets anything done."
- "My daughter has an attitude problem. She throws a fit and withdraws from us anytime things don't go her way."
- "My son is suffering from anxiety. He can hardly manage school and sports because he gets so nervous and panics."
- "My daughter is a procrastinator. She takes forever to finish the simplest task."

When I hear parents say the things above, I think one thing: *Perfectionism.* Kids who are perfectionists have an innate desire to be flawless and without fault. The problem is—you guessed it—every single one of us "falls short of the glory of God" (Romans 3:23). This means that a perfectionist is never able to obtain their heart's desire.

I think many people assume that they can spot a perfectionist by their perfection. Perfect behavior, perfect grades, perfect responses. Perfect.

But that's not true. You can spot a perfectionist by their actions: They either overachieve or underachieve. Both result in behavior that interrupts the family and stands in the way of a child's success. So how can you speak to your perfectionist child in a way that will reach through the issues to her heart? Here are a few ways to disciple your not-so-perfect child:

- **Remind your child that God created him imperfect.** Read the following verses with your child:

o "For who is God, but the LORD? And who is a rock, except our God?—the God who equipped me with strength and made my way blameless. He made my feet like the feet of a deer and set me secure on the heights" (Psalm 18:31–33 ESV).

o "But he said to me, 'My grace is sufficient for you, for my power is made perfect in weakness'" (2 Corinthians 12:9 ESV).

o "For all have sinned and fall short of the glory of God" (Romans 3:23 ESV).

Amen! What a confidence boost those words are to a soul that is struggling with feelings of inadequacy and fear of failure. We have the God of the universe, the Perfect One, going before us and blazing our path.

- **Infuse his spirit with the fact that he's not perfect, but that's okay.** No, your child won't write a perfect English paper. And your son likely won't play a perfect soccer game. And even your daughter's much-recited ballet recital won't end in perfection. But that's okay. Because God is there equipping, empowering, and helping them to find their glory in Him. So write a list about all of the ways your child is beautifully and wonderfully made—with talents and gifts and struggles—and read it to your child. Then note that perfection isn't on that list and there is a reason. Your kid was fearfully and wonderfully made (Psalm 139:14) but not perfectly made. And that is all part of His plan.

- **Read about all of those not-so-perfect characters in the Bible.** Peter denied Jesus three times. Jonah ran away from God. Rahab was a prostitute. Ruth was conniving. John doubted God's provision. Paul persecuted

God's people. Yet God used these people in powerful ways for his kingdom. Had these warriors of the faith shut down or gotten anxious after they had failed, God would have never been able to use them in the way He did. The same goes for your kids.

PRACTICAL IDEAS FOR DEALING WITH A PERFECTIONIST

Not that we are sufficient in ourselves to claim anything as coming from us, but our sufficiency is from God.

2 CORINTHIANS 3:5 (ESV)

We aren't perfect.

Have I said that enough times?

Just for good measure, I'll say it again: We are not perfect.

The problem is that kids like Alisa and Carrie don't realize this and it causes them to spin in circles, to stress, to get anxious, to overachieve, to give up. And this is okay. Because while we are not perfect—none of us—He is. And while we will never be able to do things perfectly, He can.

Without Him, we are all big hot messes. But with Him? We are exactly who He created us to be. Here are a few ideas to help your little perfectionists:

1. Don't Believe Their Words
Pillar: Desire

A perfectionist will use phrases like *I don't care* or *I can't do it* as a smoke screen to hide deep fear and discouragement. Don't believe them! (But also don't chastise your kid for saying they don't care. That will only contribute to their anxiety and desire to please and cause more inner turmoil in their spirits.)

A kid who says, "I don't care" really means "I'm scared to care," and a kid who says, "I can't" really means "I'm afraid I won't be able to." The key here is to reorder her desires—to help her to desire trying more than to desire getting it right. To desire the refinement of her own character more than the grade she gets on a project. When kids place their hopes and desires in the end result, it increases anxiety, especially for the perfectionist who sees all the obstacles in the way.

In a nutshell: We are responsible for what we do along the way, but God is responsible for the outcome.

I suggest using a clear, affirmative statement that leaves no room for argument but that gives hope to a child who is feeling anxious. Here are a few ideas:

- "Oh, Sarah, we both know that's not true! One of the reasons I admire you so much is because you care so much. Do you want to talk about why you felt like you needed to say that?"
- "The kid who was able to score six soccer goals in his game last weekend is certainly not going to let a few long division problems stand in the way, is he? Let's talk about why you're feeling that way."
- "I'm guessing God would get a good laugh out of you saying you can't right now. After all, he says we can do all things, and I believe him. Shall we pray about why you're feeling that way?"

These phrases leave no room for argument—all kids argue when they are feeling cornered—and open the door to a meaningful conversation where you can hopefully get past the "I can't" and move on to them actually trying.

2. Teach Them to Find Their Identity in the One Who Is Perfect
Pillar: Connection

When Alisa was in college, I watched God use the goal that had mattered most to her throughout her childhood—a swim scholarship to the University of Texas—to move her identity in performance to one rooted in Him. After a successful freshman year in which she broke a Big 12 conference record, Alisa came down with a debilitating illness that lasted for the next two years. No matter how hard she tried, her body would not perform. She was in her worst nightmare: She had reached her goal (a swim scholarship) but for two years, she was unable to carry out her team's expectations.

But did that mean she had failed?

I thank her coach to this day for not only selecting Alisa as team captain in that difficult season, but also for speaking truth to her by saying, "Swimming does not define you. It is merely going back and forth in the water." In the midst of a high-powered swim program, this woman illustrated grace to Alisa, breaking down the misconceived image she held of herself. She never connected her performance in swimming to her value as a person. Instead, she shared a life-changing message with my daughter: She had worth despite her ability to perform.

Prior to this, Alisa had sought, and tried to set, her worth by how well she swam. But this definition failed her. Only God can define who we are, and He will not fail us. Guide your kids not to set or seek their own worth because our own definitions will fail. We are each fearfully and wonderfully made (Psalm 139:14), and God in His wisdom created us with faults along with our strengths so that we would turn to Him. He is present in our weakness and shows up in our faults. That is how His glory is unveiled. That is the truth that set Alisa free from perfectionism.

Try saying things like:

- Our joy is in Him who never, ever fails. Happiness and contentment will never come from our own accomplishments. (See Psalm 147: 10–11)
- "You have been so faithful to study every night this week for history. Whatever grade you get, I'm proud of your hard work."
- "We all struggle sometimes. This just shows us what we can work on next time."
- "I know you can do anything because He gives you the strength." (See Philippians 4:13)
- "I love you so much. You are so compassionate and so funny."
- "I'm very proud of the good grade you got on your science project, but you know what makes me even more proud? The great attitude you showed as you worked so hard on it."
- "Oh, how our Creator loves you. He says that He draws near to the brokenhearted and saves the crushed in spirit." (See Psalm 34:18)

3. Focus on Improvement, Not on Mistakes
Pillar: Growth

A perfectionist's greatest fear is making a mistake, so when you point out the mistakes—even if she spelled the word *friend* wrong or thought 2 + 2 = 6—she's going to shut down.

Instead, intentionally point out improvement as often as possible. In doing so, you are placing the focus on growth, which is the aim of discipleship. Try phrases like:

- "A few weeks ago, you got more than half of these times tables wrong on the first try. Today you hardly missed any."
- "Wow! You worked so efficiently today. Let's go grab some hot cocoa and snuggle on the couch before bed since we have some extra time."
- "Do you realize that two months ago, this book would have been too hard for you? Look how beautifully you are reading it now."
- "I've loved watching you learn your lines for the class play. They seem so natural coming from your lips now."
- "You've worked so hard to perfect that jump shot. I'm not surprised at all that you scored six points in today's game."
- "Oh, whoops! We both missed that problem. Let's erase it and try again."
- "I can see God working so much in your heart right now. Thank you for allowing yourself to be molded by Him."

4. Set Reasonable Goals, Not Perfect Ones
Pillar: Growth

A perfectionist's inner goal is always to be perfect.

And while they may be hiding that from the world under a shroud of overachievement or underachievement, that goal of perfection is always there. A perfectionist may say, "I want to be an Olympic swimmer and break the world record" and then feel bad or want to quit when he gets second place. Or, on the flip side, a perfectionist may push all of his inner goals aside, hiding them from others for fear that they would judge him if he didn't make them.

If your child is a perfectionist, the key is to work with him to set reasonable, character-based goals instead of dream-big, success-based goals:

- Instead of "I want to be a professional basketball player," try "I want to practice for twenty minutes every day on my dribbling and passing."
- Instead of "I want to get 100 percent in math class," try "I want to turn in every assignment on time."
- Instead of "I want to get the lead in the school musical," try "I want to join the church choir so I can get more practice on my singing."
- Instead of "I want to be the best reader in my class," try "I want to read two stories to my brother every day so I can get lots of practice and also spend time with him."
- Instead of "I want to be a best-selling author of Christian fiction," try "I want to read my Bible every day so that I can know His heart."

5. Don't Get into a Battle
Pillar: Connection

Getting back to the story of Carrie from the beginning of this chapter, my last word of advice is not to get into a battle with a perfectionist. You won't win. And you will probably end up looking, well, less than perfect. If your child is refusing to do homework, don't argue with her. Don't beg, don't plead, and certainly don't do it for her.

It may sound harsh, but your kid's schooling is their responsibility and thus, ultimately, if they choose not to do the work, they are the ones who will suffer the consequences. I know that letting go of this control is one of the hardest things we can do as parents, but the truth is you can't force a kid to do their work when they don't want to. Getting into a battle with your kid will only serve to make them angry and you frustrated. I know that this could result in your kid getting a bad grade (which isn't the end of the world in third grade and would teach a valuable lesson) or even failing a class (which, again, is tough but not life-altering). Your kid's character is more important than their grades. So instead of forcing, begging, pleading, or bribing, try saying something like this and then letting your kid make the decision as to what they are going to do:

- "I hope your teacher doesn't grade you down too much for missed or late assignments. If you decide you need help, I'll be in the kitchen doing the dishes."
- "I'm sorry you don't want to do your work tonight. Would you like me to wake you up early in the morning to do it?"
- "That's your decision not to finish your science project tonight. I assume you have calculated the effect this will have on your grade in the class? I would hate for you to have to take chemistry again next year."
- "I didn't like math when I was your age either, but boy am I glad I suffered through! I use it almost every day in my job now. Who knew?"
- "I sometimes wonder if Jesus ever felt like He didn't want to do certain parts of His job either. Want to look in the Bible and see if that sort of thing ever happened to him?" (Note: It happens in the Garden of Gethsemane, Luke 22:44.)

GAINING FAITH IN GOD

Overcoming perfectionism—and thus, over issues like procrastination and anxiety—is really all about trusting God and His plan for us instead of trusting ourselves to figure it all out. When we know that it's Him we can trust, it becomes a lot easier to let go of that control and let Him do his thing.

It's always interesting to me that the kids who struggle the most in this area are often the ones who cling to God the tightest once they learn to let Jesus have control.

———

Dear Jesus,

I want to lift up Joe and Carrie and all of the other parents who are facing similar homework battles right now. Lord, fill these sweet children with a sense of wholeness, of goodness, and of righteousness regardless of their performance. Help them to find their true identity in You and You alone so that they can walk forward confidently in whatever endeavors that You have set forth for them. Help them to see that a math problem or an English paper is just a tiny glimmer of the amazing spiritual gifts and talents that You have blessed them with. Let your light shine through them, Jesus, in big ways and in small. Amen.

—— CHAPTER 5 ——

Give Thanks with a Grateful Heart

(ERIN)

And whatever you do, in word or deed, do everything in the name
of the Lord Jesus, giving thanks to God the Father through Him.
COLOSSIANS 3:17 (ESV)

MY KIDS GOT SUPER LUCKY and got to go to a really expensive, really amazing summer camp this summer. Now, there are two reasons that I say they are lucky: The first is because the camp had all sorts of amazing things like horseback riding and canoeing and waterslides and a giant blob that rocketed them high into the air before plunging them into the lake. It was amazing.

But the second reason they are lucky is that I was able to pay for it.

We don't have loads of money just lying around waiting to be spent on things like horseback riding and canoeing and water sliding and giant blobbing, so when my kids approached me about this camp, I told them we would have to wait and see if we could afford it. A few weeks later when there was an information night, we went, just to get the scoop. There, they had a preregistration where you could reserve a spot in the camp week you wanted and if you did so, you got a T-shirt.

My kids were convinced that they needed that T-shirt. So, after receiving adequate promises that you could change your registration if you changed your mind, I signed them up for week seven with stern warnings that I could still change my mind and this wasn't a guarantee of campership.

Note: I'm not really a reader of the fine print.

If I were, I would have known that starting on the day I preregistered, the camp was going to auto-withdraw $214.94 out of my account on the first of every month in order to pre-pay my kids' camp tuition.

I'm also not the most diligent with checking my bank account.

And so, come April when I sat my husband down to talk about the realities of actually sending them to camp, I noticed something strange: Their accounts were listed as paid in full.

As you can see, they got very, very lucky.

Looking back, I'm super glad it happened that way. We didn't have to scrape together $2,000 to send them to camp (since the camp kindly budgeted for me) and they had the best week of their lives doing all of that horseback riding and canoeing and water sliding and blobbing.

But then the kids got even luckier.

Since camp wasn't really on my radar when I planned our family vacation this year, we made plans to go hike in the Rocky Mountain National Park as a family. We left two days after they got back from camp. When it came down to it, they spent the entire month of July participating in jet-setting, laughter-filled, exciting, sugar-fueled fun.

Luckiest kids ever, right?

I think so.

But on the day we got back from Colorado, they made it really clear that they felt quite differently.

I will give them a teensy bit of slack: They were tired. And cranky. But still, when my simple request to bring their laundry downstairs was followed by an angsty, "Ugh...all I ever do is work!" I about lost my mind. And again, later, when another request to feed the animals was met with whining about how "we never get to do anything fun."

There's just something about kids who are ungrateful that drives me (and all parents) crazy.

Especially when that ungrateful attitude comes from camp-going, jet-setting kids whom God has blessed with pretty much the most amazing life.

To be fair, my kids are normally really great. Normally they say *please* and *thank you* and help out around the house and are grateful for the wonderful things they have. But not always.

After their little ungrateful fits, my temptation was to go sign myself up for a camp in the woods so that I could horseback ride and canoe and waterslide and blob my feelings away. And after getting letters like the one I got from my friend Allison, I know that I'm not the only one to feel that way:

Dear Erin,

I stayed up until 2:00 a.m. this morning to make my daughter a skirt for dance camp.

Normally we just find costumes from the things we have lying around at home but when I saw that the dress theme was "sailor," I immediately remembered an idea I had seen on Pinterest so I decided to surprise Madison.

So after she went to bed, I headed to Hobby Lobby and purchased blue and white striped material and stayed up really late sewing the cute little skirt, complete with slits in the front.

I was exhausted, but also excited to surprise her! I woke her up with the skirt in my hand. But instead of being excited, she

acted dismayed. She told me that she was just going to wear one
of the skirts she already had.

To be honest, I didn't respond in the best way. I was so mad! I
insisted that she wear it even if she didn't want to and that she tell
me thank you to boot. Which she did, but with a terrible attitude.

She used to be excited, and happy, with most anything new
I got for her. Now she has pretty strong opinions. Additionally,
she shows no appreciation for my effort or expense on anything.
Instead, she ungratefully tosses the things she doesn't want aside
as if she is owed nice clothes and things.

What should I do? I hate the idea of my daughter acting
ungrateful!

Allison

Well, whether it's clothes or shoes or fancy camps, it seems like our very privileged, very fortunate, very blessed kids sometimes need to learn about gratitude. So how do we fix it?

Dear Allison,

My very lucky kids can act so ungrateful and unapprecia-
tive. And what's worse, it seems like the more they get, the
more they seem to think they should get. What a cycle it is!

To be fair to our kids—both mine and yours—they are
kids. I sat mine down last week and talked to them about grati-
tude and it was amazing what one conversation did to change
things. It's like they just needed the habit of ungratefulness
to be broken. With just a little bit of discipleship—and some
prayer—our kids can flip this attitude and start showing how
grateful they are for the many blessings they have. Let me show
you what I mean.

Sincerely,
Erin

BIG PICTURE THEMES

- Gratefulness
- Thankfulness
- Kindness
- Respect
- Appreciation
- Recognition

DISCIPLESHIP FOR AN UNGRATEFUL CHILD

Not that I am speaking of being in need, for I have learned in whatever situation I am to be content.

PHILIPPIANS 4:11 (ESV)

Every November we get all excited about Thankfulness. Anyone else? We break out the "Give Thanks" napkins and put a white paper tablecloth on the table with some markers where everyone can jot down the things they are thankful for. We say prayers of thanksgiving. We talk about gratitude. We do thankfulness really, really well.

For one day.

But then on Black Friday, that thankfulness tablecloth along with everything it represents gets stuffed in the fall décor bin with our pumpkin spice candles and forgotten in a flurry of Christmas lights and 50 percent off sales.

It's not that thankfulness isn't important but simply that we forget to be thankful.

I want to point something out here: I said *we*.

Yes, my kids forget to be grateful (hence, the camp incident), but so do I. I get busy and distracted and oftentimes forget to show my own gratitude to those who make my life better and, more importantly, to the God who created me and blessed me so much. And so, in our case—and I'm guessing for several of you as well—I feel like discipleship in gratitude needs to be a family affair. Here's how we got to thinking gratefully as a family:

- **Start off breakfast each morning or dinner each evening with a conversation about gratitude.** Go around the table and have each person say a few things they are grateful for that day. You may have to set an example for your kids (who, if they are anything like mine, will say things like "Legos" and "football cards" the first few nights) and show them how to really consider what they are grateful for. For example, talk about how you are grateful that God blessed you with a spouse who supports you when you need it most or how He blessed you with children who always bring joy at moments when you are down.

- **Focus on what is going right.** How often do we as adults focus on what is going wrong? We somehow think that by focusing on our pain, we are addressing it and freeing ourselves from it. But often this focus on the negative merely serves to flood us with emotions such as fear, anger, despair, frustration, or shame. The more intensely we feel these emotions, the less aware we become of God's presence in our lives. In 1 Thessalonians 5:18, we are told to give thanks in all circumstances. By choosing to give thanks in the midst of absolutely everything (notice it does not say *for* everything but *in* everything), we find our way back to Him, who is able to restore our hearts and minds to peace and lead us back to solid footing and clear thinking. In short, we need to practice making God's presence natural to us in the midst of our pain and teach our kids to do the same.

- **Teach your kids to go to prayer in *everything* with a thankful heart.** There's that word *everything* again. In Philippians 4:6, Paul tells us not to be anxious but to trust everything to Him through prayer *with* thanksgiving. When you see a lack of gratitude in your child, turn first to prayer. Pull him aside and pray together, letting thankfulness invade every word.
- **Model thankful prayer for your kids.** Let them watch you turn to prayer in the midst of an argument with your spouse or a disappointing encounter with a friend or when you receive difficult news. Show them what thankfulness looks like.

    It's so easy to simply make prayer about our needs and concerns. Yet, when we are "watchful in it with thanksgiving," we align our hearts and minds to His will in everything we do. What a gift we have to be able to bring the mind of Christ to all our circumstances, a door we open by being thankful in the midst of our prayers.

PRACTICAL SOLUTIONS FOR A CHILD WHO ACTS UNGRATEFUL

Every good gift and every perfect gift is from above, coming down from the Father of lights with whom there is no variation or shadow due to change.

JAMES 1:17 (ESV)

I know the temptation well: When my kids act ungrateful, I want to take everything away.

All the privileges.

All the toys.

All the treats.

All the everything.

Which was why after my kids' bratty responses after their lovely week at camp and in the Colorado Rockies, my initial temptation was to just take it all away. You know, tell them that if they were going to act like that, they would never, ever so much as set foot in a camp again and all family vacations were canceled for the rest of our lives. Oh yeah, and ice cream was officially banned from our house.

But that wasn't practical.

Because I am absolutely obsessed with Rocky Road.

Oh, and because I kind of want to go on vacation sometime again.

So I had to come up with some ideas to teach my kids to react with gratitude. Here are some of the things I came up with:

1. Use Natural Consequences
Pillar: Desire

My friend Jessica told me the story about a time when she hosted her nieces and nephews for a "cousin fun" weekend. She said they had spent Saturday morning at the pool, after which they went to pizza and an arcade, followed by ice cream. Then they had gone home to rest before going to an outdoor concert. Just as my friend sat down to open a book while the kids rested, her ten-year-old nephew came downstairs and said, "I'm so bored!"

Two minutes later, the rest of the kids joined him.

The final straw came when they stood there as a group at the end of her bed with arms crossed and said, "We thought this was supposed to be a fun weekend."

My friend lost it.

And said things she regretted.

I can totally relate. I have done the same thing many times. But what does that do? It just causes more issues, more angst, more anger, and probably more ungratefulness.

So the key for when your kids are ungrateful is this: simply ignore it. Shrug. Walk away. And, of course, when you walk away, take all the treats and special stuff with you. When Jessica's crew whined about the quiet time, she simply said, "Okay, be bored. I'm going to read," and then chose not to take them to the concert that night. After all, if they didn't think swimming and an arcade and pizza was fun, why should she plan anything else?

And I encourage the same for you.

Kids often learn a whole lot more from the words you don't say than the ones you do. Instead of ranting and raving and telling your kids they need to learn to be grateful, try doing the opposite. Say something calm. Let it go. And let your actions do the talking.

2. Help Them Empathize
Pillar: Connection

After the camp incident—the one where I probably said way too many words when I shouldn't have—I decided to try a different tactic. I told them to leave their laundry upstairs. Then I called a family meeting.

"We need to talk," I started. I went on to describe how their rude words hurt my feelings. I talked about how hard I had worked to get them ready for camp, how excited I had been for them to go, how many months I spent planning the vacation and how much time and effort I put into packing. Yes, I laid it on thick.

Because I wanted them to get a glimpse of life from my perspective.

To feel empathy.

It's hard to feel grateful when we don't really understand the effort or motivation that went into something. We don't understand how others worked to help us have something or how much money they spent.

Remember Allison at the beginning of the chapter? She had spent all night sewing a skirt for her daughter. But did her daughter know that? Maybe not. Perhaps her daughter assumed that the skirt was something that her mother had found. Or perhaps she assumed it was easy to make. These are incorrect assumptions, of course, but Madison easily could have made them.

Try teaching your kids to consider others' feelings before making assumptions. Teach them to pause before they say something and consider who their words will affect. Teach them to think about the time and effort that people put into things.

After I explained to my kids all of the effort I had put into their camp and their vacation, they all immediately apologized. My ten-year-old said, "Wow, Mom, I'm really sorry. I really do appreciate this and you, and I was just not thinking when I was talking earlier."

I pray that mine are all learning to consider and empathize. And to be grateful for the efforts of others.

3. Make a Practice of Showing Appreciation
Pillar: Growth

Sometimes growing a grateful heart is as simple as practicing having a grateful heart. So make sure that attitudes of gratitude are practiced on a daily basis in your household. Here are some easy-to-implement ideas:

1. Make it a habit to write thank-you notes. For gifts, of course, but also just to say thanks for a kindness or to show appreciation.

2. Go around the table each evening and ask everyone to thank somebody for something they did that blessed them.

3. Send your kid to school with teacher appreciation gifts—a bouquet of flowers, a batch of homemade cookies, a cup of coffee.

4. Thank your kids for the things they do—for helping you with the dishes or for being kind to each other.

5. Start a thankfulness journal and jot down the things you are thankful for. Encourage your kids to do the same.

6. Replace ungrateful attitudes with grateful ones. For example, if you're feeling ungrateful about the rainy weather, say something like, "I was grumbling about the rain but then I remembered that it is really healthy for our land, and so I am grateful."

7. Start a thankfulness wall or bulletin board in your house. Remember that thankfulness tablecloth we get out every Thanksgiving? We've now decided that it's going to be a year-round thing. We sanded off the texture on one of the walls in my office and painted it with chalkboard paint. Now we encourage the kids to write or draw anything they are thankful for on the board. We also jot down Bible verses, songs, and quotes that make us feel thankful.

8. Include thankfulness to God in all of your prayers.

INCREASING GRATITUDE

I think all kids get a case of the me-me-me's sometimes.

They start to believe that they deserve the things that they have instead of realizing that our loving, merciful Father gifted us with so much more than we deserve or could even ask for.

It's a symptom of our abundance—but also a symptom of our hearts. The good news is that we serve a Father who forgives us readily and who blesses us in spite of our deservedness.

Which means we owe Him gratitude all the more.

Gratitude to God is recognizing that He is our gift-giver, and by practicing a grateful mind-set each and every day, it will become a habit that is life changing.

I pray that each of us (myself included) will develop a new sense of overwhelming gratitude for the gifts that God has bestowed on us, as well as a sense of gratitude for the amazing worldly blessings that we have: Family. Friends. Food. Shelter. Warmth. Love. Country. Hope. And a God who loves us enough to redeem us through His grace.

———————

Dear Jesus,

I know that You have blessed me with so much more than I deserve. And through trials and tribulations, through thick and thin, through good and bad, I want to turn to You and say thank you. Thank you for my rich life, full of abundance and mercy, and my redemption that comes only through Your grace. I am grateful. And I pray that I—and my entire family—learn to approach You with a humble, willing, and grateful heart.

Amen.

CHAPTER 6

Drifting Apart

(ELLEN)

Fathers, do not provoke your children to anger, but bring them up in the discipline and instruction of the Lord.

EPHESIANS 6:4 (ESV)

A MOM NAMED SARAH CAME into my office. She shut the door behind her and scooted her chair close to my desk. Then in a whisper she asked me for the name of a counselor for her eighth-grade daughter Isabella.

"Do you mind me asking what's going on with Isabella that you think she needs a counselor, Sarah?" I asked.

"Something has happened to her! She no longer wants to talk to me. She runs into her room and slams the door behind her each time I give her any direction. I hardly know my own daughter anymore." Then the tears started rolling. I knew this mother well. She had previously enjoyed such a sweet relationship with Isabella. With two brothers at home, Isabella had always been her mom's shopping partner and pedicure partner.

I hear similar laments from parents on a regular basis—especially parents with kids in the eleven to fourteen age bracket. They feel like communication has fallen apart. Their kids no longer seem to have any interest in schoolwork or athletics or drama or dance. They leave a trail of belongings everywhere they go, seemingly without caring about organization or stewardship. They yell and scream and roll their eyes but refuse to enter into logical, rational conversation with their loved ones. Parents come into my office in tears because their energetic, fun-loving kids have become sullen and withdrawn, spending more time sulking in their rooms than doing the things they once loved.

I wish I could reach out through the pages of this book with a big hug and a glass of Texas sweet tea for each and every one of you who is dealing with a bad case of teen (or preteen) angst!

It's tough to watch our kids struggle—especially when they struggle in such rude, snarly ways. And it happens so fast— one moment your precious child is snuggling next to you on the couch telling you the names of each one of her forty-three Beanie Boos, and then what seems like five minutes later, she is hidden in her room, sulking and sullen and refusing to tell you why.

Does it help—even a little—if I tell you it's normal?

Preteens and young teens are flailing for independence. Somewhere around ten or eleven their brains mature (yes, mature) to a place where they start to think logically and problem solve in a meaningful way. (Yes, they can do this earlier, but around ten or eleven, this skill becomes defined and focused. Hence, why many schools move kids into the "school of logic" or middle school at this age.)

Naturally, the first problem their brains want to solve is how to get more freedom. They are ready to be away from the restraints of childhood. They want to make choices, to figure things out, to decide on their own. And, sadly, it's often their well-meaning parents who suffer because of this internal struggle.

This doesn't mean you have to just bite your tongue and suffer through the angst! There is a balance to be struck between giving your kids the independence they crave while keeping the boundaries they need in place to keep them safe and healthy. That's what this chapter is about: how to help your preteen and young teen to grow into their God-given logical brain while maintaining your sanity and your relationship with them.

There's good news too! Most adolescents actually do want to have a good relationship with their parents—even if they won't admit it. They want to find that balance between independence and boundaries just as much as you do—they just struggle to express their needs in a way that doesn't cause problems. For example, here's an e-mail I recently received from a soon-to-be ninth grader:

Dear Mrs. Schuknecht,

Would it be possible to come talk with you about how I can get along better with my dad? I love him very much and we have been very close until this year. I know that it is partly my fault because I stay away from him. I wish he knew how much I want to be close but I no longer tell him anything that is bothering me because if I do, he lectures me and won't stop worrying. Sometimes I just want to tell him what I'm feeling but he takes it way too seriously.

Mostly, I want my dad to know that I still love him but I am no longer his five-year-old princess. I want to be trusted and treated like I am fourteen. I am trustworthy! I love God and I want to do what's right. I am getting good grades and I'm not doing anything that he would disapprove of. Okay, one thing: I've been listening to the country radio station on Pandora. I know that would really bother my dad because he thinks I should only listen to Christian music, but I love the music and I've never heard anything bad in any of the songs.

Anyway, I want to be given the chance to prove myself but I feel like they just throw a bunch of rules at me and don't think about how I feel. I feel like he thinks I have no brain and no ability to think for myself. Now I tend to keep quiet when he is around. I know that hurts him but it keeps me from getting angrier or exploding at him.

Grace

Wow! When I first read that letter, my heart ached for sweet Grace, who was intuitive enough to seek restoration in her relationship with her dad! What a great kid. But my heart also ached for her dad, who, in his effort to maintain a connected and influential relationship with his daughter, had ended up hurting the girl he loved so much. Here's my response to Grace:

Dear Grace,

Before I say anything else, I want you to know how pleased I was to receive your e-mail. I love that you care about your relationship with your dad and that you want to be close to him. Sounds like your dad wants to be close to you too!

I would love to invite you into my office to talk to me about some ideas. Do you want to meet alone with me or would you like to invite your parents to join us? I can reassure your dad and give him some simple ideas on how to make it easier for you to talk with him.

Let me know when in your schedule you have time to meet. I look forward to chatting with you.

Mrs. Schuknecht

BIG PICTURE THEMES

- Connection
- Communication
- Self-control
- Patience
- Empathy
- Understanding

DISCIPLESHIP DURING BATTLES WITH YOUR KIDS

Jesus Christ is the same yesterday and today and forever.

HEBREWS 13:8 (ESV)

After Grace wrote her lovely letter about building her relationship with her father, I met with both her and her parents on several occasions. The first time, I explained to Grace's parents that Grace had reached out to me not because she was angry or rebelling or had a problem, but simply because she wanted to figure out how to build a stronger, more solid relationship with them.

I wish you could have seen the looks of sheer relief on their faces. They, too, desperately wanted to make things right between Grace and themselves.

The first thing I did was ask Grace to express what was really going on in her heart. I told them that the first step was open, honest communication where anger and fear couldn't stand in the way. So Grace took a deep breath and looked her dad in the eyes and told him she no longer wanted to be treated like a four-year-old. She wanted freedom to choose her own radio station, her own movies, and her own friends. She wanted him to trust her. She reassured him that she was trustworthy.

I watched her father's expression as she talked. There were

several times that he opened his mouth and closed it again. Where he swallowed words he wanted to say. He later admitted to me that it was hard for him to let go of these rules. At one point he asked me, "Why shouldn't she listen to good praise music?" and I reminded him that it wasn't about what she should do. It was about what she liked. As a general rule of thumb, if your kid is asking to do something that isn't going to bring harm to anyone—herself or others—you should probably strongly consider saying yes.

Was Grace's love of country music hurting her? Nope. She had already told me that the music didn't contain bad language or bad themes.

Was Grace's love of country music hurting anyone else? Not really, except for maybe her father, who said the twangy-twang made his ears ring. But she was using headphones, so that solved that issue.

Then he had no reason to say no.

Had she asked to listen to music that had swear words or negative themes, it would have been a different story. But in this case, I suggested he say yes.

This tiny allowance on the part of Grace's dad helped their relationship greatly.

We continued to talk through the issues for a few weeks. Six months later, Grace came to me with a smile on her face. "Mrs. Schuknecht, my dad and I are getting along great! He is really trying to listen to me and hear me, and I'm trying not to get all emotional with him." I gave her a hug and wiped away a little tear, because I knew that the battle Grace had forged now would pay big dividends in the future.

Her relationship with her dad had been saved.

I have a few ideas that might help you as you try to navigate your child pressing the boundaries of independence:

- **Be on your kid's team.** The Bible says that it brings utter destruction when we don't get along with our kids. I'm not kidding. Read Malachi 4:6 (ESV): "And he will turn the hearts of fathers to their children and the hearts of children to their fathers, lest I come and strike the land with a decree of utter destruction." I don't think this was meant to frighten us but simply to remind us that God calls us to be our kids' protectors as well as their allies and comforters. It's a tendency many of us have to take an oppositional position when our kids are acting angsty or sullen or defiant. To look at it as us against them. Grace's parents noticed she was listening to country music and said no. They got angry when she withdrew. Instead, let your kids know that you are on their team. That you won't give up on them. That they can slam their door a million times and you will open it right back up a million and one. You, together with your kids, are the defenders of your family. Avoid the destruction of a broken relationship and press into your child, even if she is pulling away.
- **Check your words when you are talking to your child.** Proverbs 18:21 says that death and life are in the power of our tongues. I know that when my kids were young—especially my passionate and emotional oldest daughter, Erin—I often found myself berating and criticizing her instead of using my words to speak life into her. I remember a time when she rolled her eyes at me and said, "Whatever, Mom." I responded by yelling right back at her. When your kid snarls at you, resist the urge to yell or criticize; instead, prayerfully approach him with life-giving conversation. (Which, by the way, doesn't mean you allow the disrespect, only that you make sure your words are respectful so that he can respond likewise.) If you find

yourself battling with a kid who seems to withdraw further from you every time you speak, try changing your words:

- o Instead of "What were you thinking?" try "I'm trying to understand what's driving your actions right now. Can you help me?"
- o Instead of "Why would you be feeling upset about that?" try "I can tell you are really upset. Can you explain what you are feeling?"
- o Instead of "You are being such a brat," try "I know you! This doesn't seem like the person you want to become. What can I do to help you?"
- o Instead of "Stay away from me if you are going to act like that," try "I really don't like being around you when you are acting disrespectful. Can we try to have this conversation in a more respectful way?"
- o Instead of "If you roll your eyes one more time, you're grounded!" try "It really hurts my feelings when you roll your eyes at me. It makes me feel like we are misunderstanding each other. Let's each share what we really are trying to say."
- o Instead of "You are so angry and sullen recently," try "I can tell you are struggling. What can we do to solve this?"

- **Trust your kid.** With so many kids like Isabella and Grace, I find that their sullen withdrawal from their parents has little to do with the rules in their household or even a preteen rebellion, but instead with how their parents treat them as if they aren't trustworthy or capable. They are battling for independence and autonomy, while their parents continue to treat them like pretty little princes and princesses. Proverbs 1:4–5 (ESV) tells us to "give prudence to the simple, knowledge and discretion to the youth. Let the wise hear and increase in learning, and the one who understands obtain guidance." Basically, your kid needs some freedom. I know, I know, you don't think she's ready and she slammed the door in your face last Saturday and hasn't said a respectful word since Christmas, but...yes... you need to loosen the reins. Let her decide whether she's going to do her math homework or her science homework first. Allow her to go to the movies alone with her friends. Let her pack her own backpack and pay the consequences if she misses something. Say yes next time you have the urge to say no. Start seeing your kid as a growing, thriving soon-to-be independent adult who, dare I say, will likely make great choices if given the chance.

PRACTICAL SOLUTIONS DURING BATTLES WITH YOUR KIDS

You hypocrite, first take the log out of your own eye, and then you will see clearly to take the speck out of your brother's eye.

MATTHEW 7:5 (ESV)

Remember Sarah and Isabella from earlier?

As I talked to Sarah more, she told me that much to her surprise, the middle school years with Isabella were smooth sailing. She worked hard and had many interests. She hung out with a solid group of friends. She joked with the family at dinnertime and happily participated in family game night every Sunday evening.

But about halfway through eighth grade, everything seemed to fall apart in a matter of weeks. Sarah told about the time that Isabella had been invited to go to a soccer game with some friends and she had declined. She told her that she just wanted to stay home. This was out of character for her, but her parents had blown it off, deciding that maybe she wasn't feeling well. But that Sunday night, she refused to participate in family game night. She stopped participating in her youth group. Then, in mid-March, two of her teachers had approached her with concerns over how despondent she appeared in class. Her grades had fallen. Nothing seemed to interest her, where before she had been so excited about things. In the mornings she complained about going to school, when before she had happily popped out of bed.

What's more, if Sarah asked her once close confidante of a daughter what was wrong, she just grumbled and moped away. She seemed to show no interest in talking to her parents or siblings anymore, and even if they forced her to join the family for dinner, she said little. Sarah had no idea what to do about it, but she knew one thing for sure: She wanted her sweet, fun-loving daughter back.

I did give her the name of a counselor—I firmly believe that Christian counseling can be a great asset to parents navigating the tough preteen and teen years—but I also gave her a few ideas to try.

1. Don't Buy the Lie That Your Kid Doesn't Care
Pillar: Connection

One of the things Sarah had told me was that Isabella was refusing to go to youth group. She had told her mom that she "just didn't like it anymore" and that "she had no friends there anyway."

Red flag alert!

I asked Sarah what she did about that and she said she was making her go anyway. Sarah figured that Isabella was just in a phase and she would start liking it again. I dug a bit further and found out that Sarah had been involved in a dynamic youth group as a teenager. She had been mentored by a youth pastor who had helped her to grow a deep, abiding faith. No wonder she wanted her daughter to go!

One of the biggest lies parents believe about their kids is that they don't care. Sarah assumed Isabella just didn't like youth group but she'd get over it. But when she went home and asked Isabella to tell her more about her resistance to youth group, she found out there had been a conflict between some of the girls and Isabella was feeling isolated and alone while there.

I tell parents that anytime they hear "I don't care" or "I just don't like it anymore" about something that their kid once loved, their alarm bells should go off. Because in preteen and teen speak, "I don't care" really means "I care a whole lot and I am so upset that I don't even know how to express my feelings about this thing." Take the words *I don't care* as a sign that you should press further—in a very delicate, empathetic, and compassionate way.

Please note that in many cases, "I don't care" signifies deep hurt for your child, so it may take some time for the full truth to be revealed. Be patient. Allow your child space to talk, but also space to process and consider. Let your child know you are there when he needs to talk. Offer to connect him with a counselor or a pastor (yes, that's right, if your child needs help, you don't have to be the only person to help him).

And pray. For hope. For compassion. For healing of her spirit.

2. Parent from a Place of Hope
Pillar: Growth

When Sarah came to my office that day, she came to me from a place of fear. She was scared that her sweet, confident daughter had a major issue and would never be the same again. She felt like Isabella had completely changed and was no longer the child she had raised. She worried she had lost her daughter.

She was, of course, wrong.

God has a great plan for our kids!

Even if they are slamming doors and throwing little preteen angst tantrums, there is still hope! But—isn't there always a but?—this is a time when we as parents have to prayerfully (and honestly) assess our own motives. Are you, like Grace's dad who wanted her to listen to Christian music, trying to make your child's desires match your own? Or are you encouraging her own gifts, talents, and desires so that God's plan for your child can take flight?

At this point in your parenting career, you likely have a good idea of your child's unique God-given gifts, talents, and strengths. Go write them down. Yes, really, go get a piece of paper and write the list. I'm sure it will be long.

Now reread the list.

Do you feel that little swell of hope rising in your chest?

Yes, God has given your child a long list of wonderful attributes that will help her do great and wonderful things for His kingdom. But these attributes are still stretching and growing and finding their way in your child's little soul—and that's going to cause some bumps and bruises.

Keep this list. Read it again and again—especially after a particularly difficult day—and allow it to motivate your parenting decisions. Look forward to the hope of what is to come with your child and not to the issues of today.

Because today is but a blip.

And your child has lots of time to grow into the person God made him to be.

3. Let Them Try on Different Identities
Pillar: Desire

My grandson Joey has long hair. Think California surfer boy with little tendrils that curl out behind his ears. He looks pretty darn handsome to me, but my very conservative mother is not very impressed with his hairstyle.

"You know, I could cut it for free," she said to me. "I just get a bowl out of the cupboard and trim everything that's sticking out."

I laughed, imagining what my handsome grandson would look like then. "Maybe Joey doesn't want his hair cut, Mom."

Her jaw dropped. "Of course he wants it cut. Only the bad boys have long hair."

Thankfully, I have been able to keep Joey away from his great-grandmother's ambitious scissors, but I haven't been able to convince my mom that Joey's hairstyle has nothing to do with who he is as a person. It just reflects his style of hair. The thing about kids this age is that they like to try on new identities to see if they fit. One day they may be a California surfer boy. The next week they may become a buzz-cut-wearing jock. Later, they may decide to dye their hair purple.

As parents, we have to always ask the question: Does this hurt them or others? Does the haircut or clothing or piercing or makeup cause them to stumble in their faith? Hurt them with their teachers or employers? Pose a potential health risk? If the answer is yes, then you can say no. But if the answer is no—even if their hairstyle or clothes or ear piercing is way outside of your style or comfort zone—you may want to consider saying yes.

We have to make our relationship with our preteens and teens less about what they do—their clothes, their performance at the soccer game, their decision to wear all black—and more about who they are. We run the risk of misunderstanding and angst over trivial things like a math grade or a pair of shoes when we make our relationship about their actions. And guess what: When you're dealing with a preteen or teen, you will lose that battle.

So instead, focus on who they are. On who God made them to be. Fill your words with inspiration and hope for who they are becoming. When they come home from school, instead of asking, "How was your day?" ask "Who were you today?" By asking "Who God made you" questions, you will get some interesting, deep, and heartfelt answers—and most of all, it will ensure you don't end up in a fight over the organization of her binder.

DRIFTING TOWARD EACH OTHER

Yes, kids tend to drift away from their parents in the preteen and early teen phase. And yes, it can be a time of angst and rebellion and struggle. But it doesn't have to be. Instead, it can be a time of growth and blossoming, a time of closeness and maturing, a time of hope and joy. It's up to you.

So press into your child—hold on tight and refuse to let go (in a totally nonsmothery, cool parent type of way). Give your child someone to turn to when the topsy-turvy emotions of adolescence get to be too much.

———

Heavenly Father,

Thank you for Isabella and Grace and all of the other kids out there who are stretching and growing into the people that You made them to be. Lord, give them wings to fly high and courage to take risks and most of all, fill them with Your love so that they know they are cradled into the hand of the Most High King. Amen.

———— CHAPTER 7 ————

When Shame Takes Over

(ERIN)

He will again have compassion on us; He will tread our iniquities underfoot. You will cast all our sins into the depth of the sea.

MICAH 7:19 (ESV)

MY 10-YEAR-OLD SON JOEY SHOOK me awake at two in the morning.

"Mom!" His voice was shaky. "I had a nightmare."

I sat up in bed and pulled him down for a hug and realized his heart was pounding a million thumps a minute, his palms were sweaty, and he was shaking. He was clearly very upset.

I rolled over and climbed out of bed and grabbed his hand and led him out into the living room. We sat on the couch, the room dark, the moon glowing through the window and I rubbed his back and encouraged him to take deep breaths as he shook and sobbed. I prayed out loud for him, pleading with Jesus to take away his fear. But he kept crying, shaking, and moaning. It took more than an hour for him to settle down enough to talk or go back to sleep.

The next day—once the sun was up and the day was bright—I asked him why he had gotten so upset. I imagined a nightmare with monsters and villains and thunder booming in a dark, scary place.

But what Joey described was much more frightening.

He told me he had dreamed that he had walked downstairs in the morning to find me packing the car. He told me he had stood at the door and watched as I loaded suitcases and boxes into the trunk. I then turned and buckled his siblings into the car. In the dream, he had run out and asked me where I was going. I turned to him, shrugged, and said, "We're leaving you. I've decided to take my good kids and move somewhere else so we don't have to be around you anymore."

Ouch.

I started crying when I heard this. Big, wet, sloppy tears that I could hardly get around the lump in my throat.

My baby was scared I was going to abandon him.

I grabbed him and pulled him close and reassured him that it was just a dream and that I would never just pack up and abandon him like that. He shuddered in my arms and then told me that he knew it was just a dream.

I didn't know what to do, so I let it go.

Then he had the same dream again the next night.

This time, after an hour of tears and trembling, I called my mom. What had I done to make my son so scared I was going to abandon him? Why was he questioning his place in the family? How could I help him have confidence that I loved him? No matter what?

My mom guessed—correctly—that Joey's nightmares were caused by shame. He had been acting rude and argumentative for a few weeks, and the night before his first nightmare, he had lashed out at me after I had asked him to help me clear the table.

"Why do I always have to be the one to do all the chores?"

he had shouted. "I wish I didn't live here and lived somewhere else where parents were actually nice."

He had stormed off.

An hour later when things had calmed down, we talked. He apologized and told me that he had screamed out of anger and hadn't meant what he said. It was a feeling that I know well—I also tend to lash out and say things I regret when I'm angry.

I forgave him.

And I forgot.

But he didn't.

Instead, he ruminated on that incident all night as he was falling asleep, chastising himself for saying mean words, worrying that I was still mad.

And then the nightmares started.

This shame cycle is another thing I understand well. After I make a mistake, I can't stop thinking about it. And worrying about it. I know I am forgiven, but I don't forgive myself. My son and I are very similar. It's good, because I can understand where he's coming from and hopefully help him through it.

There are others out there who internalize their mistakes and allow shame to creep in. People who allow that shame to become a bigger influence than grace in their lives, and it causes all sorts of issues. Here's a letter about shame I received this week:

Dear Erin,

A few weeks ago, my twelve-year-old daughter Juliette turned down chocolate cake at her brother's birthday party. I passed out the slices and she said a very polite "No, thank you!" instead of taking what is usually her favorite treat. I asked her about it later and she said she just didn't feel like cake. A few days later, we pulled into Starbucks and she just ordered water, as opposed to her usual snack of mini vanilla scones. And then yesterday, she quietly removed the homemade chocolate chip cookies from her lunch.

Now I know this makes me sound like a crazy mom—I'm complaining that my daughter isn't eating sugar—but I'm worried. It's not like her to turn down treats. And it's certainly not like her to do it for several days in a row. I asked her if she was feeling okay, and she burst into tears. She ran into my arms, her shoulders trembling, and said, "Mom! I can't eat treats for two months!" I asked her why and she said she was punishing herself.

A few weeks before she had been caught lying. Her father and I had given her a pretty harsh consequence—she wasn't allowed to go to the movies with her friends—and had involved her in several long conversations about honesty. She had cried and asked for forgiveness and we had readily given it. We assumed the incident was over—but we had assumed wrong.

Juliette had lain in her bed awake for hours that night, filled with shame for what she did. She had tossed and turned and finally, she decided to give herself another consequence—no sweets for two months. Talk about willpower!

To be honest, I hate that she is so filled with shame. Sure, she made a mistake, but she has had a consequence. She doesn't need to be giving herself more. God has forgiven her, but she simply can't forgive herself.

What can I do to help her get over this?

Best,

Heather

Oh, how my heart breaks for Juliette. I have also battled shame. And those long nights awake feeling isolated and unforgiven are pure torture. What's more, this type of shame isn't from the Lord. He calls us to step forward in grace and hope, never in shame. Here's how I responded to Heather:

Dear Heather,

Similar to Juliette, I tend to wallow in my shame. When I do something wrong, I allow my thoughts to spiral. I convince myself that I have made the one unforgivable mistake and that because of that, I am somehow tainted.

It's clear to me that Juliette—much like Joey and me— is very emotionally perceptive. She is also very sensitive. So when she does something wrong, she internalizes it very quickly and the guilt and shame step in. This is a good thing and a bad thing. The good is that she clearly cares deeply about doing what is right. Her heart is in the right place. But it's also bad. God doesn't call us to a life of shame. We all have sinned and fallen short of the glory of God, but we are also all candidates for His reconciliation. And that's why shame is so damaging.

For sensitive kids like Joey and Juliette, shame can stand in the way of healthy emotional development and hinder our spiritual walk, so as parents, we have to find ways to help them stop the shame cycle and forgive themselves. I have a few ideas.

With hope,
Erin

DISCIPLESHIP FOR THE SHAME-DRIVEN CHILD

We destroy arguments and every lofty opinion raised against the knowledge of God, and take every thought captive to obey Christ, being ready to punish every disobedience, when your obedience is complete.

2 CORINTHIANS 10:5–6 (ESV)

I remember being asked to memorize 2 Corinthians 10:5 back in high school when my youth group was doing a series on sin. We were told to take our thoughts captive from issues like lust and anger and gossip so that we could keep our thoughts and our relationship with Christ pure.

This is true.

We should take our thoughts captive when it comes to issues like lust and anger and gossip. But I now believe that Paul's words were meant to go much deeper and span much further than just a short list of sins. Paul says that our weapons against the sin of the world are not of the flesh. They are of God. Then he goes on to say that we should take every thought captive to obey Christ in order to be obedient to Him. As humans, we've taken that to mean very public sins like lust and anger and we have left out other, quieter, more acidic sins like shame. Here are a few ideas:

- **Take shame captive.** In Romans 8:1, we learn that there is no condemnation in Christ. None. Which means that while we all sin and fall short of the glory of God on a regular basis, there is no place for shame. Joey's outburst after I asked him to help with the dishes had been fully forgiven by me and by Christ, but he was still wallowing in shame. As a result, he was having nightmares. I reminded him that shame is a sin just like dishonesty or angry outbursts. So he needed to tell his mind to just stop. To push that shame out. To not allow it into his heart.

- **Talk about what condemnation is.** After we talked about taking our shame captive, I reread Romans 8:1 to Joey and we talked about how there is no condemnation for those who are in Christ. I asked him if he knew what "no condemnation" meant, and we dug deeper into the idea of crime and punishment. About how it is akin to a guilty man being set free, his slate wiped clean. That's what Christ does for us.

- **Consider the trustworthiness of the Bible.** Joey needed to hear that he could fully trust God's words and apply them to his own life. We went on to talk about how when he started noticing that his mind was filling with shame, he had to turn his thoughts away and pray that Jesus would fill his mind with things that were good, true, and beautiful. Because shame is a lie. Shame is what the devil wants us to feel when we have made a mistake. But it's not from Jesus and therefore we can't trust it.

PRACTICAL SOLUTIONS FOR DEALING WITH SHAME

I acknowledged my sin to you, and I did not cover my iniquity;
I said, "I will confess my transgressions to the Lord," and you
forgave the iniquity of my sin.

PSALM 32:5 (ESV)

Shame is a quiet, internal sin.

Sometimes—I'd venture to say oftentimes—kids are filled with shame and we don't even recognize it. When Joey started having nightmares, I had no idea he was wracked with shame. I assumed he had long forgotten the incident. I had no idea that he was lying awake at night fretting over the words he had said to me.

Because it's a quiet issue, we have to be perceptive as parents and help our kids work through the habit in order to help them to overcome shame in a way that leads to growth and hope.

1. Give Your Kids a Trick to Stop Shameful Thoughts
Pillar: Growth

A few months ago, I visited a friend at her house and noticed she was wearing a rubber band on her wrist. As we talked, her toddler came in and interrupted us. She snapped the rubber band on her wrist. A few minutes later, her toddler came in again. Another snap. Throughout the morning, she snapped it several times. I finally asked her what she was doing and she explained that she had noticed in herself a habit of grumbling and complaining. She had decided to give herself a little negative reinforcement, so every time she felt the urge to grumble and complain, she snapped her wrist. She was using a physical reminder to help her to take her thoughts captive.

I don't struggle with grumbling and complaining at this time in my life, but as I considered my friend's idea, I realized that we all likely have areas where we need to take our thoughts captive. For some it may be grumbling and complaining. For others it's lust. Still for others it's anger. And for many (like me) it's shame.

While I haven't put a rubber band on my wrist (knowing me, I'd do something silly like cut off my circulation), I do like the idea of a simple reminder to take our thoughts captive. Maybe it's a rubber band, maybe it's a simple prayer (like "Please, Jesus, take over this thought"), or maybe it's a word you say every time you feel your thoughts going rogue.

I made this suggestion to Joey and he came up with the idea of a song. His tendency is to drift into shame thinking right before he goes to bed (hence the nightmares), so he decided that every time he started thinking shameful thoughts, he would immediately replace them with the song "Amazing Grace." It has worked for him. He hasn't had a nightmare in several weeks.

2. Stop Using Shame and Guilt to Motivate Your Kids
Pillar: Desire

This next section will probably really annoy some of you.

Okay, it annoys me.

Because it's really convicting, especially for parents. As I have prayed and contemplated the idea of shame over several years, I've thought a lot about the way I parent my own kids and I realize now that probably one of my biggest parenting mistakes was trying to motivate my kids through guilt and shame.

Likewise, when I talk to parents, so many others do the same thing. Unintentionally, of course, but they find themselves spinning circles with their kids, trying to motivate them all while feeling like they are failing miserably.

When Joey and I had that incident in the kitchen—I had asked him to help me with the dishes—he had responded terribly, whining and crying and ranting about how he shouldn't have to help. But guess what? I had also responded terribly. Because instead of responding to his words, I had laid on the guilt trip.

"How do you think I feel cooking and cleaning and doing your laundry all day every day when you can't even help me with the dishes?"

Yes, I said it.

I regret it.

I know that my words didn't improve the situation. Shame is not from Him. It destroys us. It tears us apart. It demotivates us. So one of the most valuable things we can give our kids is discipleship based on hope and contentment, not on fear and shame. It's important to teach your kids that sin does produce guilt. That's why it's so important to "come clean" and confess a wrongdoing so that their hearts can be cleansed of guilt and the resulting shame. Feeling guilty means your child knows he has done something wrong, so see this as an opportunity to move toward repentance—and not shame—which is what redemption is all about. Hope can take root in a heart that has confessed and is not covering up deceit. Like John 3:20 says, "For everyone who does wicked things hates the light and does not come to the light, lest his works should be exposed." So replace your shame-driven words with words of hope and redemption. Try this:

- "I imagine you are feeling really badly about how you treated your sister. I feel badly, too, when I say things I don't mean. God already knows this and is just waiting for me to confess my sin and ask forgiveness. Would you like to confess your sin and feel better too?"

- "That sad feeling you have inside you tells me that you know what you did was wrong. That makes me glad because I know you also want to change and make better choices in the future. Did you know that the Holy Spirit within us as Christians is our helper who shows us how to make better choices and we can always pray to Him?"

- "You must have been feeling pretty frustrated to say what you did to me, but I know that you don't want to treat me with disrespect because as much as it hurts me, it hurts you to act that way too. Next time you are feeling frustrated or mad, what can you say or do instead that would be more effective? I know that neither of us likes to argue like we did."

3. Be Willing to Have Tough Conversations
Pillar: Connection

That night when Joey and I scuffled over the dishes, I didn't handle it well. His attitude was awful. But mine was too. We were both tired and ready for a relaxing evening and we both made mistakes.

Later that evening when Joey and I talked about it, I quickly told him his angry words were unacceptable and he had to stop the tantrums. He apologized. I forgave him. And we had (I assumed) moved on. But had we?

Looking back, I realize that I hadn't been willing to have the tough conversation that night. Instead, I had rushed through the conversation, doing my best to get it over with quickly. And in turn, Joey couldn't stop thinking about his mistake.

After his second nightmare, Joey and I had a real talk.

I told him how I also struggle with impulsive words.

And how they fill me with shame.

We talked about ways to control our tongues and to control our thoughts.

We talked about the time when I said equally hurtful words to my own mother and how I had felt awful about it for weeks.

That time, we had a talk that took away the shame.

I think you may be noticing a theme for this book: connected conversation. We have to talk with our kids. Notice I didn't say talk *to* our kids. I said *with* our kids. We have to be willing to spend time with them to discuss issues—big and small—and help them to navigate their own mistakes, their own thoughts, their own struggles, and their own emotions.

Only then can we truly connect with their hearts.

And only then can we walk forward in understanding.

TOSSING ASIDE SHAME

What a relief that we have no need for shame in our lives. For someone like me, who is impulsive and often speaks without thinking but who also feels intense guilt and shame when I do, this is a life-changing message. I hope that you will recognize the signs of shame in your kids before they start to struggle like my Joey did. Because only by recognizing Joey's shame and working with him to get past it was he able to accept the forgiveness that he had been offered.

And to move forward in hope.

———————

Dear Jesus,

I want to lift up Juliette and Joey and all the other kids who are battling shame-filled thoughts. Help them to know that they are fully forgiven, fully loved, and fully accepted in spite of their sins. Help them to rest safely in Your arms, even after they have made a mistake. And help us who are parenting shame-filled kids. Help us to give them the tools they need to walk forward in Your redemption. Amen.

CHAPTER 8

Slow to Anger

(ELLEN)

A man of wrath stirs up strife, and one given to anger causes much transgression.

PROVERBS 29:22 (ESV)

WHEN ERIN WAS FIFTEEN OR SO, I remember a particularly frustrating time when she seemed to get angry with me for every word I said and every little thing I did. One morning, I made waffles for her and she blew up, crying and screaming about how she hated heavy breakfasts. The next day, I made nothing for her breakfast and offered her cereal and she ranted about how she was going to be late because—wait for it—I hadn't made her breakfast.

I felt like I couldn't win.

What's more, I felt like I was living with a spoiled, demanding, ranting brat. Yes, a brat. I mean, I had made her waffles and she had gotten mad at me!

I started to get angry too.

Who was she to be rude and mean and angsty to me anyway, after all I did for her? But then it dawned on me: What if something else was triggering that anger?

I knocked on her door and sat on her bed and tentatively

started the conversation: "Erin, I've noticed you've been really angry with me every morning. Is something going on?"

The tears started.

She told me about a comment I had made a few days before about her jeans being too small and how she had felt like it signaled my disapproval of her weight. (For the record, my true feelings were just the opposite: I was proud of my beautiful daughter and had noticed she had grown and wanted to buy her some new pants.) The comment had led her to feel like she had disappointed me and from then on, every time she was around me and food, her anger sparked.

And she lost control of her emotions.

As Erin became an adult, she realized that oftentimes her anger sparked when she felt disapproval from others. She's a pleaser and if she felt someone—advertently or inadvertently—disapproved of her, she would feel angry and lose control of her emotions. So now she has learned to deal with her feelings of disapproval through approaching the person with a direct and honest conversation. It works much better than getting mad.

Parents come to me for advice quite frequently about kids who struggle with anger. Parents like Kevin, whose letter was sent to me a few weeks ago, feel desperate because the anger can be so disruptive to their households, and yet they also don't want to stifle the emotions and feelings of their kids.

Dear Ellen,

My eleven-year-old daughter, Harper, has a bad temper. She has always been very emotional but recently her anger seems to have escalated. She has wild mood swings, going from a complete meltdown to acting very sweet shortly afterward. She gets angry when told no and automatically takes a defiant stance. *She gets especially angry when told she cannot play video games or be on electronic devices. Yesterday she started to clench her hands and then threw herself on the ground screaming and kicking. She even tried to kick her mother.*

When I try to talk some sense into her, things really escalate and we both wind up saying things we wish we could take back. I really don't want to go through these explosive episodes with her. Yet I know that I need to hold firm to my guidelines and I can't let her have her way. Especially when she's a screaming, shouting mess! What's more, it's causing problems with all of her relationships. Her siblings don't want to be around her right now, and I can't say I blame them!

Please help me teach her to be slow to anger.

Sincerely,
Kevin

I don't blame Kevin for being frustrated! Harper's anger and her behavior must be creating a lot of volatility in their home and a lot of emotions from all of her family members. But there is hope for Kevin and Harper! Here's how I responded:

Dear Kevin,

I had my own highly emotional child. And it happened to be Erin, the lovely adult who I am writing this book with. When she was little, she would go from quiet and calm to steaming mad in less than 2.4 seconds. I remember a time just after Halloween. Erin had quickly eaten all of her candy while her very even-tempered and self-controlled brother Troy had saved his up, only allowing himself to eat one bite (yes, bite) of candy per day. It took him a week to eat one of those fun-sized bars. I'm sure you can imagine how this turned out. About three weeks after Halloween, Troy came into the kitchen holding a Kit Kat, making moaning noises as he relished his one bite, proclaiming its creamy goodness.

Erin lost it.

She quickly grabbed that Kit Kat out of his hands, threw it down the garbage disposal, and turned it on. And then proceeded to scream and yell about the horrors of having a little brother. For several minutes. These outbursts of temper were actually common in our house. A wrong choice in TV show (sound familiar?) or a quiet snub could cause her anger to swell.

I knew I had to teach her to control that temper before she got older or she would end up having problems with her marriage, her friends, and even her job in the future. The Bible is very clear that when we are slow to anger, we honor God. Yet trying to control someone who is highly emotional (and very angry) is next to impossible. It took a lot of work—and some trial and error—but I can say that now Erin is pretty self-controlled when it comes to her anger. She's passionate and creative and emotional, sure, but anger comes slowly, just like it should.

It took me some time and intentional parenting, but I was able to come up with some ideas to help Erin get through this quick-to-spark anger. I think some of these ideas will help you and Harper as well.

Ellen

BIG PICTURE THEMES

- Anger
- Control of the tongue
- Respect toward adults
- Treating others as you want to be treated
- Self-control

DISCIPLESHIP FOR THE CHILD WHO IS QUICK TO ANGER

Know this, my beloved brothers: Let every person be quick to hear, slow to speak, slow to anger, for the anger of man does not produce the righteousness of God.

JAMES 1:19–20 (ESV)

Kids like Harper who are highly emotional and highly creative are more apt to become "emotionally flooded." Basically, all of those feelings and emotions inundate their brains and those big emotions become the driver. Suddenly things like self-control and patience and empathy and being slow to anger are washed away as those big feelings start to feel more and more powerful.

They become almost unable to consider the impact of their actions or what others might be feeling. In other words, when Harper is angry, all rational thought is pushed aside and that anger takes over.

But notice I said *almost* unable. God did not create us to be bound by irrational emotions or feelings. And he certainly didn't create us to be unable to control our emotions. So the key here is to teach her how to stop the flood of emotions before the flood carries her away. It's not easy, but it is possible. Here are a few ways to disciple her through it:

- **Ask your kid to tell you an example of someone who is foolish.** Maybe it's a kid who chooses to smoke cigarettes even though he knows they are terrible for his health. Or maybe it's a girl who cheats on a spelling test because she didn't feel like studying. In Ecclesiastes 7:9, we read "Be not quick in your spirit to become angry, for anger lodges in the heart of fools." Explain to your child that uncontrolled anger is foolish—similar to the other examples of being a fool. Tell them that by choosing to control their anger, they are choosing to seek wisdom instead.

- **Remember if anger has ever worked well.** Ask your child to give you examples of when anger has worked well for her—like when losing her temper caused her to get exactly what she wanted. I highly doubt she will find any good examples. Then discuss alternatives to the anger that so easily flares up.

- **Go through the Bible together and find examples of anger.** There are some examples of righteous anger (see Mark 3:5 or John 2:2–17 to read about some times when Jesus got angry) but many examples of unrighteous anger (see Judges 16, Psalm 37:8, Proverbs 15:18). Compare and contrast the situations and how the people responded to their anger. The conclusion you will likely come to is that anger isn't bad, but our reactions to it often are. What an important conversation for us to have with our kids!

- **Take that anger captive.** In 2 Corinthians 10:5 we are admonished to "destroy arguments and every lofty opinion raised against the knowledge of God, and take every thought captive to obey Christ." In Philippians 4:8 we are encouraged to think about those things that are true, honorable, just, pure, lovely, and commendable. This is especially pertinent to people who struggle to control their anger. Talk to your kids about how their thoughts can trigger that flood of emotions that causes them to lose their temper. Thoughts like "that's not fair" or "I hate that" cause emotions to flare and anger to become tumultuous. Teach her to take control of her thoughts and think things like "this isn't worth getting mad about" or "oh well," which will stop that flood of emotions in its track.

- **Come up with a set of family guidelines that are based on biblical truths for how to deal with anger.** Work together—she will be far more likely to abide by guidelines if she has some say in them—to come up with the list and use Bible verses as the framework for your guidelines. For example:

  - "A hot-tempered man stirs up strife, but he who is slow to anger quiets contention" (Proverbs 15:18 ESV). Guidance question: What can you do to make yourself slow to anger?

  - "What causes quarrels and what causes fights among you? Is it not this, that your passions are at war within you?" (James 4:1 ESV). Guidance question: Consider what motivates your heart to anger. How does this desire drive you?

  - "Let all bitterness and wrath and anger and clamor and slander be put away from you, along with all malice. Be kind to one another, tenderhearted, forgiving one another, as God in Christ forgave you" (Ephesians 4:31–32 ESV). Guidance question: What can you do when you are angry to handle it in a God-honoring fashion?

  - "Refrain from anger, and forsake wrath! Fret not yourself; it tends only to evil" (Psalm 37:8 ESV). Guidance question: Do you think anger is evil? Why or why not?

  - And the Lord said to Jonah (who was angry at God for showing compassion to the Ninevites), "Do you do well to be angry?" (see Jonah 4:4 ESV). Guidance question: Has uncontrolled anger ever worked for you except to cause further division?

PRACTICAL SOLUTIONS FOR A CHILD WHO STRUGGLES WITH TEMPER

Be angry, and do not sin; ponder in your own hearts on your beds, and be silent.

PSALM 4:4 (ESV)

But seriously, what can I do to just stop the temper tantrum? (You're thinking that, aren't you?)

Temper can be so disruptive to our families and our lives that oftentimes parents get desperate. They just want it to stop. Go away. And they are willing to do whatever it takes to get it to go away.

But making it stop without doing the hard work to keep the temper calm can make things worse in the long run. Here are my strategies for helping your child control his temper in a long-term, viable manner so that, yes, the tantrum will go away today but also won't pop up when your kid is twenty-two.

1. Wait Until the Battle Cools Off
Pillar: Growth

Learning never takes place in the heat of the battle.

I mean, when that flood of emotions has taken over your child's brain and she is seeing so much red that it feels like she is wading through a pot of spaghetti sauce, it is not the time to douse those flames. When your child is mad, let her be mad.

As I'm sure you know from your own relationships, talking when you're angry is never productive.

And trying to rationalize with a fuming eleven-year-old will only leave you frustrated and him...even more angry.

So if he does get angry, calmly lead him to another room—maybe his bedroom or the outside porch—and wait for the anger to dissipate. Gently take away the video game device. Quietly shut his bedroom door. Grab your other kid's hand and leave the room. Do not engage. Do not argue. Do not rant. Do not instill punishments. Do not.

Just wait.

But when he does calm down, that's when you help him. That's when you talk. You discuss. You strategize. You work on all of that discipleship that you know you need to work on. Many kids honestly lack the skills to respond to frustration, and meltdowns become the automatic response. While this is a problem, dealing with it mid-meltdown will always create a bigger meltdown—both theirs and yours.

Instead, wait. Discuss in hindsight what he could have done instead of melting down. Ask him what he needs from you to help him during these times. Let him know that you are on his team and want to help him not go into these meltdowns that feel just as bad, if not worse, for him as they do for you.

And then get to work on the next few strategies.

2. Identify the Sparks
Pillar: Growth

Remember the story I told you at the beginning of this chapter about Erin and the jeans and the waffles?

After that day (and the long conversation that ensued), Erin and I decided to start keeping track of the sparks that grew into flames of anger. Erin wrote the word *sparks* in red on a piece of paper and surrounded the word with bright orange flames. Then she started keeping track of the things that sparked her anger. Whether it was her brother doing something annoying or someone choosing the wrong TV show, she started jotting down those "sparks." Because of this record, not only were we able to start avoiding the triggers, but we were also able to identify the things—such as a feeling of disapproval—that sparked anger so that we could figure out strategies to deal with it.

Similarly, Harper, the girl whose dad wrote to me at the beginning of this chapter, seems to be sparked into anger when she doesn't get to play video games. So have her start writing down the spark the instant she gets mad. Have her try to articulate the one thing that sparked it and see if you can see any connections in the triggers. Pay attention to what comes before the spark. For example, Harper may not be getting angry when she doesn't get her choice of video games, but instead, the anger may spark when she feels unheard or disrespected.

Look for the root feeling, write it down, start contemplating it. Then you can start with idea number three, which is learning ways to douse those sparks before they become flames.

3. Find Ways to Put Out the Sparks
Pillar: Desire

Like I said earlier, oftentimes a child who easily loses her temper is a child who gets flooded with big emotions. So once you have identified the triggers to those emotions, come up with ways to squelch those sparks before they become flames of anger. It's interesting, because the desire to do right—in this case, not get out-of-control angry—often grows with experience. Basically, the more times they control an angry outburst and squelch it before it fans into flames, the more desire they will have to do it in the future.

So give your kid some tools. Write them down. Talk about them. Come up with an acronym to memorize them. Whatever it takes. Make sure your kid has an arsenal of tools to use whenever she feels a spark of anger. The same strategies won't work for every person. So discuss what works best for your child and then equip her to use them. These are some of the ideas that we had listed for my kids:

- Pray.
- Count to 10.
- Take a break.
- Stretch your back, your legs.
- Go for walk. Or if you are really angry, a jog.
- Get a glass of cool water.
- Read the Bible.
- Bite your bottom lip.
- Close your eyes and take a deep breath.
- Think about how Jesus would respond to anger like this.
- Get a snack.
- Ask for a redo.
- Ask for clarification.
- Make a wise appeal.
- Play with an animal.
- Do 10 jumping jacks.

The point is, give your kid something else to do—something helpful—at the moment when that spark flares, and hopefully they will be able to regain control of that flood of emotions before it starts to control them.

4. Tie Freedom with Responsibility
Pillar: Connection

Kids at Harper's age—okay, at most ages—want freedom. This means freedom to do whatever they want to do, to buy whatever they want to buy, to say whatever they want to say, and of course, to get their way when they want it. They want it, yes, but anyone who has spent more than four minutes with an eleven-year-old knows that giving them their own way would result in (a) doughnuts and ice cream for dinner, (b) anarchy, and (c) a cloud of glitter in your house that likely wouldn't go away until after you retired.

Clearly, most kids are not mature enough to have their own way...yet. But that doesn't mean they can't get there. I mean, none of us wants a college-aged kid calling us at 10:00 p.m. on a Friday night to ask how many cups of soap go into the washing machine. Which is why we as parents need to give them the tools they need to manage life on their own while keeping boundaries in place to keep them from getting too far off track. Basically, as parents, we have to find the balance between our kid's personal freedom and their ability to handle it.

In no area of life is the balance between freedom and responsibility more important than when it comes to personal relationships. Our kids have to learn how to deal with other people in ways that are both productive and loving. Basically, our actions should breathe life into our relationships, not pain.

In the case of a child who gets angry easily, one of the best practical ways to help a child control their anger is to put boundaries on their relationships when they lose control of their temper. For example, Kevin mentioned that Harper has had problems with her siblings when it comes to video games. My recommendation would be to set a boundary that thoughtfulness and kindness is an expectation when playing with siblings. Set up a zero-tolerance policy for fighting and angry outbursts, and no matter who is at fault, who started it, or who caused it, any violations will result in the video games being taken away.

I would likely take that one step further—that they are welcome to play video games again once they have spent time together working out a plan as to how they can play without fighting. That way, your kids can come up with a plan together—see that loving connection growing there?—and they can work together toward the common goal of being able to play video games together.

BECOMING SLOW TO ANGER

It's almost impossible to keep your cool when one of your kids is losing theirs. As parents, we know we should walk away. Take the high road. Be the bigger person. Yet when an angst-filled kid is screaming, yelling, kicking, and ranting, it takes an outright miracle for most of us to keep our cool. But, as you surely know, the worst thing you can do is get angry too.

So don't.

Instead, give your kids life-changing strategies to control that anger, and initiate conversation, dig deeper, lean into Christ, and build personal relationships that are healthy, happy, and, yes, not full of anger.

———

Dear Jesus,

Be with Harper. Fill her with the soothing water she needs to douse those sparks before they become anger. Help her to feel Your presence in those moments when her emotions threaten to flood her brain so that she is able to push back the flood and be the young woman You created her to be. And fill Kevin with patience and perseverance so he can connect with his daughter's big feelings in a real, meaningful way that helps both of them to overcome these feelings of anger.

Amen.

CHAPTER 9

Finding a Place to Belong

(ERIN)

Love one another with brotherly affection. Outdo one another in showing honor.

ROMANS 12:10 (ESV)

IT ALL STARTED BECAUSE OF summer camp.

Well, actually because of the summer camp's policy that only four kids could request to bunk together. And, yes, because I have the tendency to get a little too involved and stick my nose where I shouldn't. Because of those things, I caused a ruckus and hurt the feelings of two of the sweetest eight-year-old girls and their sweet mothers to boot.

It was completely unintentional: After I realized that my kids would be going to camp, my daughter Kate started talking to her friends about camp. Since I'm a totally chill and laid-back mom who never worries about things like my kids getting homesick and lonely at camp, I was totally ambivalent about this.... Okay, I called all of my friends and begged them to let their daughters also go to camp so Kate wouldn't be alone. I hustled and hassled and begged and pleaded until my husband came home and looked me in the eye and told me that it would be just fine.

He actually told me that I had to let go of my irrational worry and anxiety and trust God.

Rational, calm men. Sigh.

A couple of Kate's friend's moms said yes, and within two weeks, Kate was signed up in a cabin with her two girlfriends. Easy-peasy. A few weeks later, the girls somehow convinced a fourth friend that she, too, should go along—and after weeks of begging, pleading, and scheming to wear only pink for the entire week, we added a fourth member to their cabin.

The cabin was full. The pink-wearing plans had been made. All we had to do was wait.

Then I heard that a fifth girl at their school had signed up. A sweet girl named Madison who the other girls didn't know quite as well.

And Madison was in a cabin all by herself.

Enter me: The panicky, overthinking mom who felt like she just had to intervene to make sure every girl felt okay at camp. I called all of the other moms and explained the predicament and we decided as a group to move two of the other girls into Madison's cabin so that no one would be alone. Good plan, right? Well, it was. Until I heard through the grapevine that a sixth girl—Caitlin, who is a close friend of Madison's—had joined the fray. So I got all panicky and overthinky again, and we moved the girls back into their original cabin, assuming that Madison and Caitlin would be fine together.

Are you following all of that?

Long story short: In my effort to make sure all of the girls felt comfortable at camp, I made all of the girls feel weird and uncomfortable. And hurt some feelings too.

In hindsight, I should have just kept Kate in the original cabin that she signed up for and not done all of the finagling and moving and calling and talking. Because my moving and stressing and worrying and finagling caused a lot of hurt. When we got to camp, Caitlin and Madison realized that the cabins had been moved and moved back and moved again and they felt left out. By the time I realized the hurt, there was nothing I could do about it other than apologize.

I can honestly say I never meant to hurt anyone—my intentions were good, as I wanted all six girls to have the best camp experience ever. I wasn't trying to make sure my daughter had the best cabin or was with certain people. And I certainly wasn't trying to leave anyone out. My mistake wasn't intentional or malicious—my mistake was in getting overly involved in the first place.

I think many moms like me get inadvertently caught up in the crazy social dynamics of their kids' lives, and feelings and relationships are hurt in the process. We mean well! We want our kids to develop strong, fun friendships where they can learn and grow together. We want to help! But we mistakenly help in all the wrong ways.

This chapter is about how we as moms and dads can help our kids be great friends and support them as they navigate these relationships in a way that is helpful, uplifting, and God-honoring and not cause hurt and jealousy in the process. I got an e-mail about this exact type of situation just last week:

Hi Erin,

Last week, we got an e-mail from the room mom that they were planning a play date at a local park. My eight-year-old daughter Liza was so excited! She couldn't wait to hang out with her school friends on a weekend!

When we showed up at the park, I noticed that several of the girls were wearing blue T-shirts with a rainbow on them. I asked Liza about the shirts and her face fell. She explained that

"Gwen's mom made them for Gwen's friends on the first day of school. They all wear them every Friday."

My heart broke. My poor sweet daughter was one of two girls in the class who didn't have the blue shirt on.

I watched as she walked over to them to play and the girls were sweet. They included her in their game and definitely weren't being mean to her, but as Liza's mom, I couldn't help but feel like she was the outsider. Like she didn't belong.

How do I navigate this? I certainly don't want to interfere or cause a scene, but I also don't want my already quiet daughter to slink into the background as a blue-shirt-wearing clique forms. I just don't know what to do.

Beth

It kind of makes you want to go out and buy a blue shirt with a rainbow on it and ship it to Liza, doesn't it? It did for me. But then I read the letter again. Beth does say that the girls were sweet to Liza. They included her in their game and weren't mean to her. It doesn't appear that they disliked Liza or were bullying her. Instead, they had just gotten caught up in the fun of having matching blue shirts.

Hi Beth,

Your letter brought up a lot of feelings for me: First, sadness. Poor Liza! And poor you. That must have been hard to watch. But then I felt guilt. Because I have done the exact same thing that Gwen's mom did.

Last summer, Kate decided to make "school spirit" beaded necklaces as a summer project. She made them for all of her friends and they wore them together on the first day of school. I didn't even think anything of it—Kate had so much fun making the necklaces and her friends loved them. But then on the first day, I saw a new girl in their class looking at them longingly. She was the only girl in the entire class without a necklace.

I felt awful! That night, Kate happily made her a necklace and gave it to her in a little blue bag on the next school day. She immediately put it on, but the damage had likely been done: She had felt excluded on her first day of school. And it had been my fault.

Navigating our kids' social relationships in a way that allows them to grow socially all while avoiding hurt feelings is tough. We have to remember to see it from all sides. In reality, Gwen's mom likely wasn't trying to exclude Liza or make her feel left out, but instead just thought it would be fun to make shirts for the girls. And just like me, she got caught up in social engineering without thinking of the consequences.

All that said, I have a few thoughts on how to navigate these social situations with our kids. I hope this helps!

Erin

Big Picture Themes

- Friendship
- Empathy
- Kindness
- Bullying
- Understanding
- Social engineering

DISCIPLESHIP FOR KIDS LEARNING ABOUT FRIENDSHIP

Let not steadfast love and faithfulness forsake you; bind them around your neck; write them on the tablet of your heart. So you will find favor and good success in the sight of God and man.

PROVERBS 3:3–4 (ESV)

When Kate was three, she became close friends with two girls in her preschool class. Oh, how she loved Jessie and Lila! The three of them played all the time. They had so much fun together and never seemed to have any problems. Just girly giggles and hugs and baby dolls.

As we laughed at our girls' hugs and smiles, I got to know Jessie and Lila's moms. We all agreed that we wanted these precious first friendships to be special and lasting. And we wanted them to teach our kids what friendship meant. So we did our best to teach our girls about kindness and empathy and understanding and grace. We taught them that it was okay if Lila and Jessie had a play date and Kate wasn't invited and it was also okay if Kate invited one of them over and not the other. We taught them how to navigate adding new friends to the mix and how to deal with conflict. We taught them about sharing and listening and including.

I have to admit: We've been really fortunate because Kate and Lila and Jessie are about the sweetest girls in the world. They naturally just seemed to catch on to these lessons. So on that first day when Kate heard that Lila invited Jessie over for a slumber party, I was able to say, "It's okay! That doesn't mean they don't like you. It just means they wanted to have a sleepover together." Things just seem to work.

I think we all want "just seem to work" friendships for our kids. But the word *seem* is in that sentence. The truth is that Lila's and Jessie's sweet, wonderful moms have worked with me to disciple our kids into an understanding of what friendship means and how that plays out at school, at church, at home, and at the playground. Here are a few of the things we've learned:

- **Choose to serve the Lord, regardless.** In Joshua 24, Joshua is struggling to lead the stubborn Israelites into the Promised Land. Over and over again God has proven his justice and mercy. And over and over again, they have rejected Him. Yet Joshua, in all of his frustration, stands before the tribes of Israel and makes a proclamation: "As for me and my house, we will serve the Lord." Make that your mantra. Yes, those girls are being mean and excluding you, but as for us, we will serve the Lord. It can be a tough pill to swallow for kids—especially kids who feel the sting of rejection. But help your kids through it. Give them specific examples of how they can serve God even when rejected:

○ When a group of kids forms on the playground and leaves two or three out, teach your kid to walk over to those sitting on the sidelines and create their own game.

○ When your kid isn't invited to a birthday party, plan a service outing with a sibling or another friend. Allow the joy of serving others to perk up her sad spirit.

○ Share times in your life when you felt like you didn't belong (it happens to all of us) and how you learned to deal with it in a constructive manner.

○ Remind your child that being left out does not mean a failure on her part and that everyone experiences it at some point.

○ Discourage her from talking badly about friends who have left her out. Instead, write an encouraging note to a friend or family member or draw a picture for Grandma.

• **Help your child see that he belongs to the greatest "group."** Sit down with your child and read through some verses about our inclusion into the family of God. Ephesians 2:19, says that we are "members of the household of God," and 1 Peter 2:9 says we are a "royal priesthood" and a people for "His own possession." This is a chance for you to connect with your child over the fact that she is a daughter of the King. She is worth more than rubies and diamonds (Proverbs 3:15). She is exquisitely loved by the One who made all (1 John 4:7). Suddenly owning one of those blue shirts doesn't feel quite so important, does it?

- **Make family a priority.** When your kids are feeling like outsiders, it's your chance to show them that they are an insider. Circle the wagons around your family. Make family time a weekly or even daily priority. Plan movie nights, plan game nights, plan family dinners, plan a mini weekend way. Allow family time to soothe your kids' tender spirit and to remind them that they are loved and included.

PRACTICAL SOLUTIONS FOR KIDS LEARNING ABOUT FRIENDSHIP

And as you wish that others would do to you, do so to them.
                                              LUKE 6:31 (ESV)

Joey has a friend named Mark.

Mark is a great kid—he's fun and kind and generous and polite. We love having him around. Mark's family is great too. But last month, Mark's dad made a mistake. (To be fair to Mark's dad, it was an honest mistake. He wasn't trying to be mean or to hurt anyone, but we'll get to that.)

It all started with a rec league basketball team.

Mark's dad signed Mark up and volunteered to coach the team. Cool, right?

Much to my basketball coach dad's chagrin, Joey didn't want to be part of it. He didn't want to play basketball because he wanted to focus on soccer. We didn't sign him up, so we watched this story unfold from the sidelines.

In the end, seventeen kids signed up for the team. Like I said, Mark is a great kid and his dad is a fun coach. I'm not surprised so many kids wanted to be on the team. But it posed a problem for Mark's dad: He had to remove seven kids from his team. Those kids could play on another team, but they couldn't play on his. He was put in a situation similar to the one I was in with camp: There were limited spots and too many kids wanted them. No matter what, kids would be hurt.

Here's where Mark's dad made his mistake: He chose the best kids to be on his team.

Now, before you jump up and e-mail me and remind me that on high school and college teams, kids are cut all the time and that coaches have to choose the best kids, let me remind you of one thing: This is a fourth-grade recreational basketball league. It's created to be a learning experience. Mark's dad had sent an e-mail out to all of Mark's friends to ask them to join. Because of this, choosing the best kids was a mistake. An honest one, but one that brought hurt feelings to many of Mark's friends.

What could Mark's dad have done differently? Probably the same thing I should have done with camp: Let the group be comprised of those who signed up first and let the other kids form a second team. It would have avoided a lot of hurt feelings and would have made the decision objective rather than subjective.

We are all learning—Mark's dad, me, the mom who made the blue shirts—to navigate these situations—and I'm guessing 90 percent of the time, they are inadvertent even while painful. So we have to give other parents and kids a lot of grace and be very thoughtful when it comes to situations like these. Here are a few ideas to help our kids (and ourselves!) navigate tricky social situations in the future:

1. Teach Your Kid that Exclusion Isn't Rejection
Pillar: Growth

My friend and I went out to coffee the other day and she told me that growing up, her parents had a rule that everything had to be equal for all of their kids. When she told this to me, I nodded and quickly said, "That's great!" My first thought was, *What could be wrong with equal rights for all?*

She frowned at me and shook her head. "No, Erin, you don't understand. It was awful."

She told me about the time she got invited to a birthday party and wasn't allowed to go because the birthday invitation had said "no siblings please." Since her little sister hadn't been invited to a party that day, she had to decline the invite. Later, when she was in high school, she had wanted to go to the senior prom. But...you guessed it...she wasn't allowed because her little sister wasn't old enough. She said her entire childhood turned into this crazy battle to find something for her sister to do so she could have a social life.

Don't do this to your kids!

It makes things so complicated and makes them feel unwanted when they aren't included. Remember Gwen's mom—the woman who made T-shirts for some of the girls in her daughter's class? Those blue shirts were so hurtful to Liza's mom. She felt like her daughter was being excluded. And I get it. I would have felt the same way. The girls probably should have reserved their matching shirts for a time when everyone would be included.

But the flip side is that Gwen's mom simply couldn't have been expected to make a T-shirt for every kid in the class. Just like Kate couldn't have been expected to make a school spirit necklace for a new girl in her class. So then the duty falls back to Beth—Liza's mom. She has to help Liza see that she is okay, loved, and cared for even without a blue shirt.

In life, not everything is even! And it shouldn't be.

It's okay if your son wants to have a small, intimate birthday party with only four kids in attendance. It's okay if your daughter wants to make a special friendship bracelet for your closest neighbor. It's okay to have play dates and family dinners and go on outings with some kids and not invite others. It's okay to have matching shirts with a group of your best friends.

Those are all things that are part of friendship.

It's our job as parents to teach our kids to be okay with the fact that sometimes they won't be invited. Sometimes the other kids will have a play date without including them. They will have matching T-shirts or matching headbands or matching soccer cleats. They will go on a family vacation to Mexico together or have dinner at each other's houses. And this doesn't mean your kid is being rejected. Their not being invited or included to something doesn't mean they aren't liked or aren't wanted.

Teach your kid to be happy for their friends when they get invited to a slumber party. Teach your kid to not even notice the matching shirts or the friendship bracelets or the birthday party invitations. An exclusion isn't necessarily a rejection. It's just part of life and something that will happen again and again as your child grows up.

2. Don't Flaunt the Exclusions
Pillar: Growth

There will be times that you are excluded.

And there will be times that you do the excluding.

Mark's dad had to cut seven kids off the team. You can't invite the whole world to your child's birthday party. You can't buy Christmas gifts for every child your kid has ever met. Gwen's mom couldn't make blue rainbow shirts for every child in the school.

Doing the excluding isn't a bad thing, but making a big deal of it is. For example, Gwen and her friends probably shouldn't have worn the blue shirts to an all-school park play date.

Likewise, the kids on Mark's dad's basketball team probably shouldn't make sweatbands that say "We're on the A team" and wear them every day while they shoot hoops at recess. (For the record, they didn't. Mark's dad was very gracious and kind about the entire situation and the kids never flaunted their participation in the team.)

And when your kid decides to have a small, intimate birthday party with only three friends, that's fine. It's a good thing! But the kids probably shouldn't show up at school with party favors, screaming about how "epic" their weekend was.

Teach your kid to be discreet about her inclusions and quiet about exclusions so that kids' feelings are preserved.

3. Let Your Kids Choose Their Own Friends
Pillar: Connection

When I was in college, I got a summer job as a nanny for two adorable little girls. I was so excited—I was going to spend my summer playing with the cutest kids I had ever seen and I was going to get paid for it. The best part? My best girlfriend got a job as a nanny for a family that lived right down the street. We planned to meet in the neighborhood park every day for a play date.

On the first day, I laced up two pairs of shoes and took the hands of my two charges and we walked down the street to the park. When we got there, I spotted my friend across the playground and we ambled over and said hello. The kids ran to the jungle gym, only to return two minutes later in tears.

We quickly learned that the two kids we had been hired to nanny for didn't get along. Apparently the two older girls had been in the same class and had had personality clashes all year. They were both sweet, precious girls when they were separate, but together: Anger and chaos ensued. The last thing the two of them needed were play dates all summer long. So my best friend and I slunk back to our own jobs and spent the summer doing all sorts of fun things with great kids—but not with each other.

This has happened with me and my own kids as well. There are some really cool moms out there who I really love to hang out with, so naturally, I want my kids to get along with their kids. And in many cases, they do! Score! Family dinners and play dates galore! But there are times when my kids just aren't meant to be best friends with my friends' kids. Maybe it's a personality clash or a difference in interests, but for some reason, friendship is a struggle.

Does this mean you can't hang out with these people?

Of course not! Your kids need to learn to get along with all kinds of people! At certain times, you should absolutely plan family outings and dinners with people your kids don't necessarily get along with. But that doesn't mean your kid has to be best friends forever with the kids that you choose for him.

Instead, let your child make her own friends. Invite the kids over for play dates or on outings and try to get to know their moms. Let them figure out who they get along with. And let them choose who they sit by on the bus. Don't finagle relationships just because they are easy for you. Don't force relationships that aren't working. And don't make your kid hang out with someone they don't get along with.

Instead, just proceed with kindness, reminding your kids that while it's essential that they are always kind to everyone, they can choose the people they spend the most time with.

This is the lesson I learned with my camp cabin finagling

last summer. My daughter had chosen to go to camp with three of her close friends. I should have left it at that. When I found out that another girl was going, I should have reminded Kate to always include and be kind to the other girls at camp. Then I should have left it alone. I should have stuck with the original plan and allowed her to navigate her own friendships.

4. Help Your Child Build Other Friendships
Pillar: Growth

When kids are feeling left out of a group, probably the best thing you can do is help them form a new group. When Beth noticed that Liza was one of the only girls in the class without a blue shirt, she immediately assumed that Liza was being left out of the group. As parents, we may even automatically assume that the group—the girls with the blue shirts—are the "cool" kids or the ones everyone wants to be friends with.

But what about the other kids not wearing blue shirts?

Could you reach out to them?

I'm guessing that the other kids without blue shirts were feeling just as left out. While I wouldn't encourage Beth to go make green shirts to create dueling cliques, inviting a few of the non-blue-shirt kids over for a play date or outing could be a great way to help Liza make new friends.

This year in school, my daughter Kate's new class list included five girls she had never been in class with before, including Madison, the girl from camp. It wasn't that she didn't like these girls—she simply didn't know them. She had always been in class with a different group of friends, and the idea of starting over and breaking into a new friendship circle scared her. But we had a long chat and I encouraged her to see this as an opportunity.

Madison and her friends are sweet, kind, funny, precious girls. They immediately welcomed Kate in and they quickly hit it off. Within days they were laughing and joking and making plans for pool parties. They were having a great time in their new class. The best part? When Kate came home from school yesterday, she was bubbling and giddy because at recess, all of the girls—Kate's friends from before and her friends from now—played together. How's that for a happy ending?

HELPING OUR KIDS BUILD LOVING FRIENDSHIPS

When we feel left out—or worse, when our babies feel left out—those mama and papa bear claws come out. We don't like seeing our babies wearing pink shirts when all of the other girls are wearing blue. And we don't like the idea of our kids missing out on, well, anything.

But our kids do belong: Regardless of who has blue rainbow shirts and who doesn't, each of our kids was lovingly created to be part of God's family. We have a place, and it's a place where we are much loved, much wanted, and much treasured. So even as we navigate human friendship, we must remember that there is more: Because our true treasure is our spiritual family, and in that family, there will always be a place for us.

Father God,

Please reach down and help our kids to develop uplifting, strong friendships that stand the test of time. Help these friendships to be fueled by kindness and mutual understanding and never impeded by jealousy or social engineering. Give us the grace as moms to teach our kids to be great friends all while avoiding getting too involved. Amen.

CHAPTER 10

A Friend in Need

(ELLEN)

Anxiety in a man's heart weighs him down but a good word makes him glad.

PROVERBS 12:25 (ESV)

THIS IS THE CHAPTER THAT I didn't want to write.

I kept shoving it aside, writing other chapters, researching verses for other sections, pushing this one to the back of my to-do list. Until today. Today, I woke up with a new resolve that this one has to be written. Because today I got yet another phone call from another set of parents who had learned something awful: Their daughter's best friend was cutting herself.

And their daughter knew about it.

I'll get to that particular story in a little bit, but first, I want to give you a little mom-to-mom advice: Don't ignore this chapter. Don't think it couldn't happen to you. Don't say, "We raised our kids in a Christian home and my kids would never, ever hurt themselves." Too many good, loving Christian parents think those same thoughts. They think it would never happen to them, that things like cutting and self-harm and suicide are things that happen to *other* kids and *other* parents. They assume this is an issue that they will never have to worry about.

They make assumption after assumption.

And then it's too late.

I didn't want to write this chapter because it's a little too real for me, too raw. I didn't want to write this chapter because this exact issue has deeply affected families that I know and love. I didn't want to write this chapter because I knew it would dredge up a lot of pain. I knew there would be tears and a lump in my throat and an empty quiver in my stomach as I wrote it. I didn't want to remember.

But I have to.

For you, for your kids, and for the kids in your community who are struggling with this issue right now. Because we need to be able to disciple our kids through the hard stuff—the really tough, evil, angry, from-the-devil stuff. We need to band together as Christian moms and dads and support the kids who are struggling in our community. We need to have plans in place before it's too late.

I know this firsthand because it happened to us.

To my community.

To my dear friends.

A middle-school girl, from a family I worked with, committed suicide two years ago. This girl—we'll call her Dara—was raised in a wonderful, loving Christian home. She had great parents who loved her, who raised her in a home where she knew about God and love and relationships. Parents who *discipled* her. Parents who would have done anything for their daughter but who along with our community missed the signs of desperation and struggle until it was too late.

After Dara died, our community was devastated.

Kids and adults alike were wracked with guilt over the what-ifs—what if I had told someone? What if I had realized Dara was crying out for help? What if I had noticed? We brought in a team of wonderful Christian counselors to walk the community through it—and in the process, learned that Dara wasn't the only one struggling.

There were others.

Other kids who had ventured into the world of cutting and self-harm. Kids who struggled with depression and a distorted view of self-worth. Kids who were at risk for suicide. And I need to say something very important right now: If your child or a child you know is struggling with self-harm or depression or suicidal thoughts, they need immediate, qualified professional help. You need to immediately pick up the phone and call a licensed Christian counselor or a medical professional right away.

Your advice, your support, your love, this book cannot and will not be enough.

So get the help that is needed.

But this chapter isn't about those kids—it's about the other kids. The ones who are crying out about the what-ifs. The ones who know about a friend cutting or hurting themselves and don't know how to handle it. The ones who want to be good friends and advocates but need help.

This chapter is for the parents of those kids who know more than they want to and don't know what to do about it. For example, below is the story I referred to earlier:

Dear Ellen,

I knew something was wrong as I walked by my daughter Rylie's room and overheard pieces of her conversation with her close friend Tara. I heard my daughter whisper, "Roll up your sleeve," and then I heard a gasp. I heard Rylie whisper, "Why are you doing that?" and then my ears really perked up when I heard Tara say, "I will kill myself if you tell anyone."

After Tara left, I asked Rylie about it and she told me I must have misheard. Her eyes darted to the side as she said, "It's fine, Dad. Tara is fine." But I kept pressing and Rylie started to sob.

I learned that Tara had told Rylie that she had started cutting her arms with a kitchen knife because "it felt nice to release the pain." What was more, Tara had confessed to Rylie that she sometimes thought about what it would be like to die and that she had even found some pills in her mom's medicine cabinet and had wondered how many she would have to take to "just be done with it all."

My poor daughter is feeling such a burden about this! She is really worried about Tara, but she also promised her friend she wouldn't tell and she is pleading with me not to call Tara's parents. Rylie says it would betray Tara's trust and she would never be her friend again.

What should I do now?

Sincerely,
Derek

What an awful thing for Derek to overhear...but I am so glad he did. Whenever I hear stories like this, I thank God that someone found out before the child truly got hurt. Depression and self-harm are major issues that must be dealt with, and I believe that God uses incidents like Derek overhearing to get His children the help they need. Here's how I responded to Derek:

Dear Derek,

I am so glad you overheard this. While this will likely be one of the most difficult conversations you have to have with your daughter, it's also one of the most important. Tara needs help. And it sounds like you have been put in the position to give her the help she needs.

First things first, you have to tell someone immediately. No matter what Rylie promised Tara, Tara's life and health are more important. Pick up the phone and call Tara's parents immediately. If they aren't receptive, call the school or church or a counselor. Make sure that Tara does not have another opportunity to cut herself or to contemplate taking those pills.

Once you feel confident that Tara is safe, then turn to your daughter. She is likely experiencing a wide range of emotions about this situation and will need your discipleship and support more than ever as she navigates this situation. I have some ideas to help you help her to get through this.

In prayer,
Ellen

BIG PICTURE THEMES

- Self-harm
- Friendship
- Depression
- Suicide
- Confidentiality

DISCIPLESHIP FOR WHEN A FRIEND IS INVOLVED IN SELF-HARM

Rejoice in hope, be patient in tribulation, be constant in prayer.
ROMANS 12:12 (ESV)

Last year, a fifteen-year-old girl came to my office with wide eyes. I could tell something was on her mind, but she kept hemming and hawing—asking about my grandkids and talking about the weather.

I invited her in to sit down. "What's up, Vivianna?" I asked. She sighed.

Then she bit her lip and told me that she shouldn't have come, that she didn't know what she was doing there. And she left.

The next day she was back. The same thing happened.

Then again on a third day.

Finally, on the fourth day, I had a gut feeling that she was worried about a friend, so I took a leap and started talking: "Vivianna, I can tell you have something you want to tell me. I am worried that maybe you are worried that someone is going to hurt himself or herself, and I want you to know that this is one case where you can break confidentiality. We can't keep secrets when someone's health is at risk."

A tear trickled down this sweet girl's face. She pulled a well-worn letter out of her pocket and handed it to me. I carefully unfolded the piece of paper and began to read the words written in a flat, spiky font:

- You are the only reason I am still alive. If you ever break up with me, I will kill myself.
- I can't survive without you. I sometimes think about what I would do to myself if you ever weren't my girlfriend. It would be ugly.

And, perhaps the most frightening:

- I have already decided the knife I will use to split my wrists if you and I ever get into a fight.

Vivianna swallowed hard. "It's...it's Michael. I-I-I like him but my parents won't even let me go out on dates yet. I thought we were just friends who hung out sometimes at lunch and now...well, he's going to kill himself if I'm not his girl-friend? He also said he would hurt himself if I ever told anyone and now what if he finds out I told you?"

What a terrible burden for Vivianna to be carrying!

I immediately told her that she had done the right thing by telling me. I told her Michael's health is always more important than his confidentiality and I told her that by telling me, she became his advocate and the person who cared enough about him to get him the help he needed. I told her to wait in my office for me and I immediately went to the head of school's office to call for help. We called Michael's parents and our counselor.

(I'm going to stress this one more time: Even if your son or daughter or a kid who has confided in you is upset or begs you not to tell or is angry with you for telling, the first step you must take is get help for the person who needs help. Then, after that, you disciple the one who told.)

Once I knew Michael was being taken care of by a profes-sional team, I went back to Vivianna. She was still crying. I reassured her that we were helping Michael and he was going to get what he needed. I once again reaffirmed to her that she made the right choice. I asked her if she would like me to call her mom (she did) and if she wanted her mom to come in (her mom was there in ten minutes). Then, together, we talked through the following things:

- **Doing the right thing isn't always easy.** There is a myth out there that if we do the right thing, the road will be easy and flat. But that's not true. In 1 Peter 3:14, Peter tells us that "even if you should suffer for righteousness' sake, you will be blessed. Have no fear of them, nor be troubled." Vivianna's mom and I told her that while Michael may be angry with her for a time, or while she may feel guilty for breaking his confidentiality, her decision to seek help for him was the right thing. And that even if we suffer for our righteousness, we will eventually be blessed.

- **Do not allow weariness to overcome you.** We told Vivianna that there was a good chance Michael would be angry with her for a while. That she may regret that she had told or wish that she hadn't. Together, we read Galatians 6:9: "And let us not grow weary of doing good, for in due season we will reap, if we do not give up." She should stand tall knowing that Michael would be better in the long run because she had talked. And we reminded her that in due season, maybe not even in this lifetime, but in due time, all would realize that she had done what was right.

- **Read Psalms of comfort.** Even in the hardest situations, Jesus brings comfort. Together with Vivianna, we looked up several Psalms of comfort and read them aloud together. Here are a few examples:

  o "For his anger is but for a moment; and his favor is for a lifetime. Weeping may tarry for the night, but joy comes with the morning" (Psalm 30:5 ESV).

  o "He heals the brokenhearted and binds up their wounds" (Psalm 147:3 ESV).

  o "Even though I walk through the valley of the shadow of death, I will fear no evil; for you are with me; your rod and your staff, they comfort me" (Psalm 23:4 ESV).

- **Pray together for the one who is hurting.** We reminded Vivianna that the best thing she could do was pray. Right then and there, Vivianna, her mother, and I prayed for Michael. For his healing, for his hope, for his future. And that his relationship with Vivianna would be restored.

LIFE-CHANGING SOLUTIONS FOR WHEN A FRIEND IS INVOLVED IN SELF-HARM

When the cares of my heart are many, your consolations cheer my soul.

PSALM 94:19 (ESV)

An incident of potential or actual self-harm or suicide will change a campus, a family, and a community forever. I am sure that Rylie and Vivianna will be forever changed by what happened with Tara and Michael. And I know our school and community was changed forever by the death of Dara.

To be truthful, this change is God-honoring—we have to change and learn and grow in order to be sanctified. It is in situations like these that our kids can see God move in beautiful, miraculous ways.

Because of the seriousness of issues of self-harm, I changed the header in this section to "life-changing" solutions instead of "practical" solutions because I wanted to give heed to the fact that when someone is hurting themselves or planning to hurt themselves, practicality isn't what is necessary. It's a life change, a change of thinking, a change of perspective that helps heal deep wounds. And thus, in this section, I want to show you some ideas on how you can change your family's perspective or outlook in order to make sure that kids who need help get the help they need.

1. Remind Your Kid that Secret-Keeping Doesn't Equal Caring
Pillar: Connection

After Vivianna told me about Michael's letter, she worried that Michael would be angry with her. She said to me, "I really like Michael and now he's going to think I don't care about him at all because I told his secret." Kids tend to believe that keeping a secret is the best way to show someone that they care. But in cases of self-harm, it is just the opposite: If someone is going to hurt themselves, a friend who cares gets them help.

Kids like Vivianna and Rylie need to hear from parents and teachers that they are wonderful, caring friends for being willing to get help. Remind them again and again that they did the right thing, that they were very brave and courageous and that they showed their courage by telling an adult and getting their friends help. Explain that a true sign of friendship is the willingness to do the hard thing even if it means conflict or could result in the loss of a friendship.

If it helps, use the attributes of love in 1 Corinthians 13 to write out a list of attributes of a good friend and then walk through them one by one:

- You were patient when you read Michael's letter and didn't get angry or mean, but instead got worried and sad.
- You were kind when you sought out help for him even after he told you he didn't need it.
- You showed him that love bears all things when you prayed for him even after he hurt you.

Make the attributes of friendship—and the fact that your child embodied them—the center of many conversations for several months so that whenever your son or daughter starts to doubt their actions, they will have someone to remind them that they did the right thing.

2. Make a "Safety First" Policy in Your Household
Pillar: Growth

Every family should have this rule: Safety must always be valued over confidentiality. When a friend knows someone is doing things that are harmful, an adult needs to get involved. Period. No exceptions.

Tell your kids that friends who are at risk for hurting themselves will often use threats—"I will hurt myself if you tell," "I won't be your friend anymore," "I will be so angry"—to keep their secrets confidential. But in reality, they are often crying out for help. The most important thing your child can do if they think a friend is at risk is to tell an adult.

Make it your family policy that if your child comes to you with an issue of safety, you will immediately drop whatever it is you are doing to listen and help them. Promise your child that you will serve as a sounding board and help them to discern if any situation is really a safety risk. Then tell them that you will be the advocate who will step in and help whoever is in an unsafe situation get the help they need.

3. Talk About the Future
Pillar: Growth

Tara and Michael are children of God.

They have hope and a future.

Their lives are not over.

Ask your son or daughter to talk about where they see their friend who is struggling in the future. Maybe Tara wants to be a great artist or Michael plans to win the high jump at the state track meet. Have your child imagine Tara or Michael when they are twenty, thirty, and forty.

Explain how the actions of telling—of getting Tara and Michael the help they need—can be a catalyst for making that future plan a reality. Remind them that God isn't done with Tara or Michael yet and that by them getting help and support, His plans can still be fulfilled.

4. Don't Let Your Kid Take Responsibilities for the Actions of Others

Pillar: Growth

One of the things I have seen several times is children who are involved in some form of self-harm try to get others to feel responsible for their choices. For example, last year, a group of girls found out that one of their friends was using a candle lighter to burn herself. When they found out, she wrote a text message to the group and told them that she wouldn't burn herself again if they promised not to put their phones down at night so she could know she could reach them at "any time day or night."

But—she warned—if she texted and didn't get a response, then she would have no choice but to get out her lighter.

Three of her friends went into a panic, worrying that if they put their phones down to go to a movie or have a family dinner, they would miss a text and end up responsible if their friend got hurt. These girls spent several weeks worrying about their phones before one of them finally confessed what was going on to an adult.

The truth is, your child is not responsible if a friend is involved in self-harm. I like to remind kids that it takes a true professional—a doctor or a counselor with a degree and experience—to help when someone is ill. And since self-harm is an illness, someone who isn't a professional cannot be responsible for "healing" someone who has this disease. All they can be responsible for is taking their friend to an adult for help.

Your child can't be tied to her cell phone waiting for a text. And Vivianna can't be afraid to break up with Michael because he might get upset. And Rylie can't be afraid to tell her dad because Tara might cut herself.

Kids tend to assume that they can help a friend by carrying the burden and giving a listening ear. Because of this, they wind up feeling guilty if they don't make themselves available whenever the troubled friend cries out for help. This can consume them and wind up draining their energy and time and making them feel responsible to keep a friend alive or from hurting themselves. When Dara committed suicide, she left behind a circle of absolutely devastated friends, all who had tried to help her and then felt like failures. We have worked with these kids for over a year now to help them see that this wasn't their fault and that they are only responsible for their own actions—which, in the case of self-harm, means they need to tell an adult.

So first they tell an adult. Then after that, all they can do is pray and be a good friend.

DOING THE RIGHT THING WHEN IT'S HARD

I wish this chapter hadn't been necessary. That issues like self-harm and suicide weren't part of our culture and our community. But they are. In order to help kids who are struggling, the best thing we can do is talk about them and come up with community guidelines that will help kids get the help they need and to teach our kids to be advocates for their friends who need help.

Because kids like Michael and Tara are children of God.

They are important.

And their lives matter.

Dear Jesus,

There is so much pain in this world that at times it feels daunting. But You have promised that You have overcome the world! And so please overcome the hearts of Tara and Michael and other kids who are struggling with depression and self-harm. Get them the help they need and bring healing. And likewise, be with kids like Rylie and Vivianna who have made the tough choice to help their friends. Comfort their hearts and fill them with a peace that comes with knowing that You are God and You love them. Amen.

—— CHAPTER 11 ——

A Kind Word Turns Away Conflict

(ERIN)

She opens her mouth with wisdom, and the teaching of kindness is on her tongue.

PROVERBS 31:26 (ESV)

It's DEFINITELY THE CAR'S FAULT.

That's the only logical explanation since there is no possible way I can blame my three precious cherubs for the constant fighting in the car.

Every time we get in the car, without fail we have a sibling conflict. Today's fight was simple: The car has this very tempting button on the back of the seat that makes the headrest fling forward. And so, of course, little brother pressed said button. And so the soft, pillowy headrest fell forward at the rate of about .0002 miles per hour and tapped Kate on the head. And the terrible pain and drama of the headrest tapping her on the head caused her to scream. Which naturally caused big brother to join in and tap her again on the head. Which caused more screaming.

So, as you can see, it's the car's fault.

But regardless of fault, the bickering and whining and arguing and picking continues. And what that means to me is that by the time I arrive somewhere, I am on the verge of screaming. It's not all the car's fault, of course. The house is occasionally to blame as well. Someone isn't helping. Someone is making a weird clicking sound with their shirt. Someone is looking at them in an annoying way. Someone is... well, you get the picture.

If you are anything like me, you just want the sibling fights to go away. Like, seriously, disappear so we can all go back to being the sweet, happy, loving family that I know we are. But shooing them away without some serious discipleship will likely lead to more... wait for it... fighting. So instead, I'm on a mission to teach my kids to be peacemakers and resolve their conflicts in a way that doesn't include hitting, whining, or throwing a fit.

A lofty goal, I know.

But it will be worth it if I am able to drive to the grocery store listening to Garth Brooks instead of my daughter's moaning—and if my kids learn how to be peacemakers instead of peace destroyers in the process.

KIDS WHO GET THEMSELVES INTO CONFLICT

Dear Erin,

My eight- and nine-year-old daughters fight all the time. It feels like from sunup to sundown. They used to share a room and before I could even make my morning coffee, I would be hearing tales of woe about someone's clothes being all over the floor or someone kicking someone on her way to the bathroom.

We decided to move them into separate rooms, thinking it would stop the drama, but instead, it's only gotten worse.

They seem to annoy each other with every little action they each make, and they seem to intentionally pick at each other every opportunity they get.

This past weekend's drama started when my older daughter decided she wanted to try out for the soccer team. After she finished her homework, she went into the yard where she practiced by kicking the ball against the side of the house over and over. It was certainly annoying. But I gritted my teeth and put in some earplugs because I knew that was what the coach had asked them to do.

Of course, my younger daughter had none of that grin-and-bear-it attitude. Especially right when she got to the good part in her Rick Riordan novel. She threw down that book, ran outside, and calmly asked her sister to stop. The soccer-playing sibling explained that the coach wanted her to practice. The reading sister said that her teacher wanted her to read. And so it went until both were screaming at each other.

It ended with two slammed doors and two girls crying in their rooms.

I want them to be best friends, not archenemies. But I have no idea how to teach them to resolve conflicts in a reasonable way, without it escalating into a huge drama-fueled fight.

Help, please!
Emily

I couldn't have said it better myself: I want my kids to be best friends, not archenemies. Yet I get nervous that we are quickly headed down the archenemy path, as they seem to fight over every little thing. While I don't want to keep sweating the small stuff (I can't tell you how many times my daughter has gotten angry at one of her brothers for "breathing weird"), I also want to teach them to deal with issues in relationships before they explode. No drama. No anger. But a lot of good conversation.

> *Dear Emily,*
>
> *We're right at the end of summer vacation. A few days ago, I went out to lunch with some of my girlfriends. Interestingly, none of us are feeling overly excited for our kids to go back to school. We all agree that regardless of the chaos of summer, having them home in carefree, no-math-homework, stay-in-your-swimsuit-all-day oblivion is the best! Except for one thing: the fighting.*
>
> *It was universal: The six of us had nineteen children combined. Children who have wonderful gifts and personalities. Kids who are kind and thoughtful and loving and empathetic. Kids who excel in school and in sports. And yet, much to our chagrin, these nineteen delightful children had spent the entire summer fighting with their siblings.*
>
> *It is so heart-wrenching for us as moms to watch our kids bicker and fight—especially over little nitpicky things that would be so easily solved with some simple conflict-resolution skills. And so this summer, that is what I've been trying to instill in my children. In the following pages, I'll fill you in on what I did.*
>
> *Erin*

BIG PICTURE THEMES

- Conflict resolution
- Anger
- Connection
- Kindness
- Empathy
- Peacemaking

DISCIPLESHIP FOR KIDS LEARNING CONFLICT RESOLUTION

Do nothing from rivalry or conceit, but in humility count others more significant than yourselves. Let each of you look not only to his own interests, but also to the interests of others.

PHILIPPIANS 2:3–4 (ESV)

I was raised in a home where I wasn't taught healthy conflict resolution. We were taught to "be peacemakers" and "not to take offense"—which are healthy, godly principles that are often misconstrued to mean "run away and avoid conflict until you explode with anger." So that's what we did in our house growing up.

I remember one time when I was a teenager, I got angry with my parents over their rule that I couldn't do anything non-school related on a weeknight. It was seven or eight o'clock on a Wednesday night and my homework had been long finished and I wanted to walk down the street to my neighbor's house to play a board game. My parents said no with hardly a glance in my direction.

Now here's the thing: At that time, I would hardly have been known as a peacemaker. I was an exploder. I got angry and I let everyone know it. But what my parents didn't realize was that I really was trying. That night, I distinctly remember walking away from my parents and silently coaching myself to be a peacemaker. I remember telling myself it wasn't a big deal that they weren't letting me go, that it was a hard-and-fast rule so I shouldn't have even asked, that I should not take offense and that I should let it go. My parents may not have known it, but I was trying to do just that.

But the thoughts kept popping into my head.

Don't they trust me?

I'm fifteen years old and I can't go play a board game with my neighbor?

It's not like I don't get good grades.

But I pushed it aside. I did what I thought was right. And I didn't say a word. Until a night a few weeks later when my friends were going out to fro-yo. On a school night. This time instead of asking, I screamed, "Everyone is going to fro-yo and I'm stuck here in this crazy strict household."

Things didn't go well for me.

Or for my parents either, I'm guessing.

But I have to consider an important question: Had I resolved the first conflict in a way that was healthy and brought forth true peace, would the second conflict have even happened? How do I teach my kids to be true peacemakers, ones who discuss and address offense instead of fleeing and exploding?

In the last ten years or so, my parents have realized that they didn't teach us healthy communication skills. Interestingly, we've learned it's not too late. My mom and I have intentionally and pointedly worked to build these skills with each other and others. Just the other day, we had a conflict and my mom came up to my house. We spent ten minutes talking it through. She apologized, I apologized, and we moved on. I haven't thought of the issue even once since. There is no brewing anger, no explosion waiting to happen, because now we understand what being a peacemaker really means.

And we are working to teach our kids the same so that when they are teenagers they will know how to come to us and others with conflict in a way that's God-honoring and relationship-building. Here are a few ways to disciple your kids in this area:

- **Teach your kids what being a peacemaker really means.** In Matthew 5:9, we read that the Lord blesses the peacemakers. But we have to dig a bit deeper to understand what that means. In Romans 14:19, we are told to "pursue what makes for peace and for mutual upbuilding." And in James 3:18, we are told that "a harvest of righteousness is sown in peace by those who make peace." Phrases like *mutual upbuilding* and *harvest of righteousness* show me that making peace is a process—a process that allows iron to sharpen iron and in which each of us is refined by fire. Explain to your kids that true peacemakers intentionally work through conflict so that we all can be better and more like Him. God calls us to pursue relationships and reconciliation with people who have hurt us, which means often being the first one to offer the olive branch of reconciliation. So help your child to write that tough e-mail, to make that phone call, or to knock on that door and be the first to pursue peace.

- **Practice a wise appeal.** In Proverbs 24:3 (ESV) we read that "by wisdom, a house is built, and by understanding it is established." Explain to your kids that in the midst of a conflict, by showing wisdom, we are able to "build our houses" into strong fortresses in the Lord. When I was a teenager, I imagine that had I come to my parents with a calm, reasonable request—perhaps stating that I felt untrusted that they didn't let me go to my neighbor's house and that I would like them to reconsider—they would have at least reconsidered. Regardless of their decision, I am positive that a wise appeal would have expelled the anger and avoided the future issue. So teach your kids to say the words—"I heard what you said, but I would like to make a wise appeal"—and then teach them to calmly, respectfully state their case without anger. Then teach them to be okay with the results.

- **Explain what it means to not take offense.** Growing up, I believed that Proverbs 19:11 (ESV)—"Good sense makes one slow to anger, and it is his glory to overlook an offense"—meant that when something offended or upset me, I should just ignore it. But read the first half of that verse; it says that good sense makes us slow to anger. Meaning before we explode, we should learn how to settle our anger and to pursue peace with calm and understanding. Similarly, when it says "overlook an offense," I believe that means being quick to forgive and quick to assume the best in others. For example, the night my parents didn't let me go to my friend's house, I assumed it was because they didn't trust me. I was offended. Later, they told me that they had quickly said no because it was a hard-and-fast rule and it had nothing to do with trust. In choosing not to be offended, I would have quickly believed them on that and assumed the best. Not ignoring my feelings, but instead, allowing my feelings and theirs to be discussed in a peacemaking manner.

- **Give your kids peacemaking phrases to use when conflict arises.** It's hard for kids to know how to respond when they are angry or upset. Kids need to know what to say and when to say it. For us, we have a typewritten sheet in the top drawer of our craft cabinet. It has a list of phrases that my kids can use when there is a conflict. I ask my kids to go grab the sheet and read it in order to spark ideas. Here are some of the phrases on our sheet:

- "When you _____, I felt really hurt. Can we talk about it?"
- "I love you so much that I don't want there to be anger between us. Let's see if we can work this out."
- "I know that I hurt you when I _____. I want to apologize. Can we talk about it?"
- "I realize that we aren't seeing eye to eye, but I want to understand you. Can you explain why that made you so angry?"
- "I want there to be peace between us. What can I do to make that happen?"

PRACTICAL SOLUTIONS TO STOP SIBLING RIVALRY

The beginning of strife is like letting out water, so quit before the quarrel breaks out.

PROVERBS 12:17 (ESV)

Siblings fight.

I fought with my brothers and sisters.

My kids fight with each other.

And, oh, my nieces and nephews, they fight too.

For my kids, it's usually due to pesky brothers and a whining sister. The boys think it's hilarious and fun to pick on their sister. So they sing la-la-la songs, they taunt her, they grab her stuffed animals, they move her dolls. Of course, she can't just let it go and ignore it. No, she has to respond! To react! So she whines and cries and screams that she has the meanest brothers in the whole entire universe.

It's great fun for everyone.

Well, everyone except for me. I just want to start crying as well.

Looking back at my own childhood, I realize that the worst thing I can do as a mom is ignore these sibling conflicts. Yes, things like "he took my toy" and "she's not sharing" are minor issues. But they are so important if we want our kids to learn to resolve conflict in a way that's healthy. To build close, connected relationships. As a parent, fostering healthy conflict resolution with our kids and their siblings is a skill that will pay off big-time in the future. So don't ignore, don't react, and definitely don't referee, but instead, equip your kids to build healthy, connected relationships. Here's how:

1. Give Your Kids Tools to Stop Ignoring or Exploding
Pillar: Growth

Most people have one of two natural reactions to conflict: They ignore or they explode. Or both. Very few of us are blessed with the ability to resolve conflict naturally. We have to work at it. We have to overcome our natural bent to handle things in an unhealthy way.

My natural bent is to ignore the conflict until it builds up and then I explode. My daughter, Kate, is the same way. She will be kind and loving and caring with her brothers for days, overlooking myriad offenses and pouring kindness into them. I watch her with awe, thinking about her patience and empathy. And then she explodes. Out of nowhere, the dam will burst and she will scream or even hit one of her brothers. (Let's hope she never does that in school!) I'm always baffled at how she can turn from sweet and kind to angry and mean so quickly. But it's because she internalizes the conflict.

So I'm teaching her to bring small conflicts up as they happen. "Hey, Joey, when you grabbed that stuffed animal out of my hands, it startled me. Can I please have it back?" or "Hey, Will, I would love to play with you, but you are going to have to stop throwing Legos all over my room." These simple statements give the boys the power to stop the conflict and allow her not to stuff everything inside.

Likewise, my son Will is an exploder. The second something makes him mad, he blows up. Yesterday, I let him play the iPad for an hour while I worked with the other kids on their reading. When I asked him to put it up, he took one look at me and screamed, "I'm in the middle of a game" and threw the iPad across the room. It crashed into the wall and cracked the cover. (Thank goodness it didn't crack the screen.)

Needless to say, I'm teaching him how to be slow to anger. Yesterday, I handed him back the iPad and said, "That was a really angry reaction, which isn't how we behave. Let's practice doing that again the right way." Then I went back out of the room, came back in, and asked him to put the iPad up. This time he handed it to me. We talked about ways he could defuse the anger. Maybe he calmly asks for one more minute to finish the game. Maybe he takes a deep breath and tells me he's saving the game so he can finish it the next day. Maybe he closes his eyes and counts to ten. I gave him tools and ideas so he could make the right choice in the future, instead of just yelling at him for making the wrong choice. (Which, by the way, is what I was tempted to do.)

I do want to point out that there was still a consequence for throwing the iPad—he doesn't get to use the iPad for two weeks. Explosive anger is never okay, so there will be consequences for those actions. But in addition to consequences, we have to give our kids tools to avoid anger and to stay calm when they are upset.

2. Teach Your Kids Mediation Skills
Pillar: Connection

In the heat of the moment, we all need mediation skills. (Yes, including adults. I can't tell you how many times I've called another adult in to help my husband and me navigate a tough conversation. Okay, I'll tell you: a lot of times.) We have to recognize that sometimes in really difficult or long-term conflict, all of us need a mediator.

Because of this, this process is twofold: First, teach your kids to ask for a mediator if they feel like a conflict is getting too heated or emotional to handle on their own. Ask them to request someone who is kind and God-loving and who loves both people in a way that they can see both sides. If at all possible, try not to let this person be you in sibling conflicts—I've learned the hard way that if I try to mediate my kids' conflicts, I often end up as the referee and things get more emotional and heated. Instead, teach them to seek out another sibling, a cousin, a neighbor, an aunt or uncle, a grandparent, or a friend.

Second, teach your kids to be mediators. Work through the discipleship section of this chapter, making sure they understand what a peacemaker is and what God's vision is for conflict resolution. Then show them how to walk a conflict from anger to resolution by asking leading questions, listening to both sides, allowing each person to express their emotions and respond to them, and then seeking a solution to the problem. It will take time, but if your child has mediation skills, they will be able to solve their own conflicts and help others do the same.

3. Understand Each Child's Unique Personality
Pillar: Connection

Remember all that stuff we said about every child's unique and God-given personality? That means your kids are going to have conflict that is unique to their unique personalities and unique dynamic. Have I said *unique* enough times? I'm not sure. But the way my kids have conflict isn't the way your kids have conflict. Which means all of those tried-and-true rules that you have read about resolving conflict may or may not work with your kids.

Sibling conflict is one of those areas that parents have to work to gain understanding of their own children and then formulate a plan that fits each situation. It's a lot of work, but it will pay off in the long run when your kids learn healthy conflict-resolution skills.

Because your kids are different from my kids, I can't give you a step-by-step plan. I can, however, give you some ideas to get you started. Try them out next time your kids have conflict, see what works for your kids, and start helping them to build healthy relationship skills.

- **Give them a coffee talk.** You know how as an adult if you have something on your mind, you go for coffee to talk? Give your kids the same advantage. Set them up with cocoa or lemonade or water (and maybe if you are nice, cookies) and have them sit at a table facing each other—with you in the other room—until the conflict is resolved.

- **Have them write each other letters.** Ask them each to write a letter as to how they are feeling, then trade letters and have each read them. From there, have each person discuss the other person's letter—no, they don't get to rehash their own grievance but instead talk about what they understood the other person to be thinking or feeling.

- **Have them exercise while they talk.** Exercise releases endorphins, which helps us to calm down. (Yes, this works for adults too.) So have your kids head into the yard and jog side by side or do jumping jacks while they chat through a conflict.

- **Have them reach a conclusion together.** Yesterday my mom had my kids over for lunch. A few minutes into lunch, Kate whined that her brother Joey had thrown a piece of his hot dog at her. Joey immediately denied it. She sent them out on the patio and told them they were not to come back in until they had the same story. They came back a few minutes later and explained that Joey had thrown something at Kate but it was just a crumb of the bun. Kate agreed. They both apologized—Joey for throwing bread and Kate for whining and assuming it was a hot dog. The fight was over. Before you try to referee a conflict for your kids, see if they can come to a conclusion on their own and give them practice working on those powerful conflict resolution skills.

4. Make Conflict a Good Thing
Pillar: Desire

The other day, I went out for coffee with my friend Marie. She sat down and burst into tears and said, "Oh, my husband and I got into a fight again. I feel like we have a bad marriage because we fight so much." She went on to explain their nagging conflict over financial issues and how they resolved it. As

Marie and I talked, I realized something, though: Their conflict was a good thing. They actually had a very good marriage.

I listened to Marie as she shared how her husband had gotten frustrated about a financial decision and he had come to her about it. She explained how she had responded and he had addressed her concerns. Words had gotten heated but then they had come to a solution together and found reconciliation.

Marie was feeling upset because they fought often.

But hearing how they resolved this conflict with a godly, mature, Bible-based attitude made it seem like a good thing to me. I told Marie what I was thinking and she nodded. She agreed: The conflict did make them closer, and they did resolve it in a healthy way.

I think in our culture, we assume conflict is bad. We think, "Well, I never see eye to eye with so and so, so it must not be meant for us to be in relationship." But that's just wrong. I believe that unhealthy conflict is bad. Healthy conflict is not only relationship-building, but it also sanctifies us. (Remember James 3:18? Conflict brings about a "harvest of righteousness.")

So encourage your kids to look at conflict as a good thing. As an opportunity to grow closer, to consider the feelings of others, to deepen their spiritual walk and to find sanctification in the process.

RESOLVING CONFLICT

It's become clear to me that my kids are going to fight.

And it's become clear to me that this conflict is a good thing. It brings them closer to each other and to Jesus, and it gives them skills to forge healthy relationships with future friends, neighbors, and spouses. So I'm going to take my own advice and start looking at those nitpicky sibling fights as opportunities for them to grow and as opportunities for me to grow as a mom as well.

Jesus said, "Blessed are the peacemakers," and so that's my goal: Peacemaking in the way that God intended it and strong, healthy relationships as a result.

Dear Jesus,

Fill Emily and all of the other moms who are dealing with sibling conflict with Your peace. Help us to learn what it truly means to be peacemakers and to pursue that peace in all of our relationships. Give us a desire to resolve conflict and help us to recognize our own tendencies to ignore issues or to explode and instead, help us to resolve conflict in a way that honors our relationships and more importantly, honors You.

Amen.

─── CHAPTER 12 ───

Free to Be Modest

(ELLEN)

For you were called to freedom, brothers. Only do not use your freedom as an opportunity for the flesh, but through love serve one another.

GALATIANS 5:13 (ESV)

LAST SUMMER, WE HAD SOME FRIENDS OVER to swim in our family pool. The friends had an eight-year-old daughter who was wearing what looked like a wet suit when she arrived. Jennifer, the girl's mom, walked over to me and said, "I had to go to the store to buy Faith a new swimsuit this morning because I didn't want her to be seen by the boys wearing a regular swimsuit. I had to explain to her that boys look at women's skin and can think of nothing else so it's our job as godly women to make sure we stay well covered."

I stood there for a few minutes thinking about what Jennifer had said. The more I thought about it, the more it upset me. Her comment made me realize something I had been contemplating for a long time: Our Christian culture has taken the godly value of modesty and turned it into something very ungodly. And moms like Jennifer and girls like

Faith get trapped trying to meet a standard that is unequivocally flawed.

A standard that makes women responsible for how men behave.

A standard that causes boys to feel like they can't be trusted to do the right thing.

And a standard that causes little girls to worry about things they never should be worried about.

Modesty is a hard issue to navigate because it is both a godly virtue and a source of legalism in our culture. As parents, we have to help our sons and daughters find the balance and get to a place where modesty is linked with a desire to do right by God and to honor those around us. Let's read what Erica had to say about this topic:

> *Dear Ellen,*
>
> *I just spotted a picture of a young girl on Facebook. When I first saw it, I immediately thought, "Wow, that looks like my Emily! Except that girl's parents let her out of the house wearing next to nothing. I would never allow that." Then I looked a little closer. Sure enough, it was my Emily, standing with her arms around two guys, wearing a pair of tight jeans with a blue T-shirt that showed about six inches of belly. On top of that, she had her lips painted dark blue and dark black eyeliner on her eyes, making her look harsh and cold and nothing like the beautiful, smart, and kind girl that we raised.*
>
> *I showed it to my husband and we both started to cry. We have worked so hard to instill values like modesty and humility into our girls. To see Emily dressed like that makes me feel like we have completely and utterly failed. I have half a mind to go through her closet to see what else she has hiding in there. Oh, and then replace every item with a Puritan-style dress.*

What do we do now to keep our beautiful, smart daughter dressing more modestly without our house erupting into a war zone?

Sincerely,
Erica

I remember watching my own daughters leave the house for school and second-guessing myself and our family's standards of modesty. I had beautiful daughters and there were so many times that I just wasn't sure where to draw the line. Additionally, it's hard to find the fine line between allowing kids to find their sense of style and sticking to a standard of modesty. Here's what I said to Erica:

Dear Erica,

Oh boy! I can't tell you how often I get calls from moms and dads about this very issue. At our school, we have a very conservative uniform and even then, I often catch girls unbuttoning an extra button or rolling the top of their skirt to make it a little shorter. And, like you, I feel so sad for these girls who have bought into the lie that their attractiveness stems from showing too much skin instead of from who they are.

As parents, we walk a very fine line when it comes to the issue of modesty. We can't control our kids. Even if we were to buy all Puritan dresses for our daughters (which, I admit, would be my first impulse as well), we still probably couldn't ensure that our daughters would wear them. There are always friends who are willing to loan clothes. Or malls that have sales. And even if you somehow managed to force Emily to wear the clothes you want her to, she will be going to college in the near future. I highly doubt you'll be able to show up to her dorm room to check her skirt length before she heads to class in the morning.

So the key here is to teach Emily to value modesty on her own—in a way that demonstrates that you are her advocate and support system, not her judge. It's a tough job. But I have a few ideas.

Good luck!
Ellen

BIG PICTURE THEMES

- Modesty
- Humility
- Inner beauty
- Attraction
- Courtship

- Opposite-sex relationships
- Money
- Sneaking around
- Control

DISCIPLESHIP FOR OUR KIDS ON THE ISSUE OF MODESTY

So flee youthful passions and pursue righteousness, faith, love, and peace, along with those who call on the Lord from a pure heart.

2 TIMOTHY 2:22 (ESV)

Our kids get so many mixed messages when it comes to modesty. While the Bible calls on women to focus on their internal beauty and their godly virtues, the secular media is telling those same women to show as much skin as possible, all while the Christian culture is telling them things like:

- "It's your job to make sure to stay covered so men won't think about the wrong things."
- "All men will think about is your skin if you are showing too much."
- "Even at the age of eight, boys will be looking at you as a sexual being if you wear clothes that reveal too much."
- "Men are unable to control themselves if they see a woman wearing clothes that are immodest."

I hate what these statements say to our daughters, but I hate even more what they say to our sons. Our daughters hear messages about sexuality, physical attractiveness, and lust. Then they hear that they have the power to keep men from sinning. At the same time, our sons hear that they are somehow incapable of self-control and that it's not their fault if they feel lustful if the woman is wearing the wrong clothes.

It's wrong. I think we as a Christian community need to rethink modesty—not by swinging toward secular values and wearing risqué clothing, but by looking at the root of the issue and trying to change our kids and our culture from the inside out. Here are a few ideas:

- **Focus on your son.** My friend—a youth pastor—tells the story about how he walked into the church one day for youth group and found one of the high school girls wearing tight low-rise jeans, a low-cut top, and bright pink lipstick. The rest of the girls were wearing the typical youth group uniform of maxi-skirts and loose tops. He said he watched as the boys walked into the church assembly hall and one by one made their way over to the girl in the jeans. Within ten minutes, there was a cluster of girls standing by the water fountain giggling amongst themselves while the boys were huddled around blue-jean-and-lipstick girl while she told a story. The truth is that we don't know exactly what was happening here. The girl wearing the jeans may not have even realized she was dressed immodestly. And possibly, the boys noticed things like the lipstick more than they noticed the low-cut shirt. But this story does illustrate that boys are naturally drawn to girls who dress a certain way. And while this is a natural God-given thing (God created men to appreciate the way women look!), it's something that we as parents need to be aware of. Because while sexuality inside of marriage is good and holy, sexuality in the youth group is not. The fact stands: If we want our daughters to learn to dress respectfully, we have to teach our sons to be respectful to girls when they are dressed modestly.

- **Teach your kids of both genders the values of modesty and purity.** God created sexual attraction and beauty for a reason. The goal can't be to change our son's natural, God-given attraction to beautiful women or to hide the beauty that our daughters were blessed with, but instead to teach them about God's values of modesty and purity. Read the following Bible verses about modesty and beauty and love:

  o "Since we have these promises, beloved, let us cleanse ourselves from every defilement of body and spirit, bringing holiness to completion in the fear of God" (2 Corinthians 7:1 ESV).
  o "But each person is tempted when he is lured and enticed by his own desire" (James 1:14 ESV).
  o "But put on the Lord Jesus Christ, and make no provision for the flesh, to gratify its desires" (Romans 13:14 ESV).

PRACTICAL SOLUTIONS TO HELP OUR KIDS BE MODEST

How can a young man keep his way pure? By guarding it according to your word.

PSALM 119:9 (ESV)

Like I said earlier, modesty is a tough issue because it's overvalued in some communities and undervalued in others. Because of this, our kids are given a series of mixed messages that are not only confusing, but also lead them to easily be influenced toward cultural norms that don't hold with their own personal values. To overcome this, we as parents need to help our kids—both boys and girls—seek God's values and to work to align their own values with His.

1. Be Your Daughter's Advocate, Not Her Judge
Pillar: Connection

Has anyone ever advised you to never be your kid's friend?

I know I heard that statement a hundred times when I was raising my kids. Well-meaning people (and books!) explained that if I was going to be a disciplinarian and a teacher, I could never be my kids' friends. But I wholeheartedly disagree. Because while there is a time and a place for discipline and instruction, there is also a place for advocacy and friendship, which are foundational for discipleship.

When a big issue comes up in your kid's life—think alcohol, cheating, drugs, or sex—do you think he will turn to the person who has been a source of discipline or to the person who has listened to him and advocated for him his entire life? I think that's clear. By intentionally and lovingly listening to our kids as they grow as Christians and as humans, we can grow a trusting relationship where they know they can tell us any-thing without being judged. When they trust us, they will turn to us when the stakes are high.

There is, of course, a fine line. You have to be a friend and advocate who listens without judging but who also holds to a standard. It's a tough job, but it starts when you intentionally spend time talking with your kids and listening to what they say without jumping to conclusions or judging their words.

As far as modesty goes, before you can even begin to influ-ence your daughter's clothing choices, you have to intentionally work to get to know the reasons behind her clothing choices. Make it your aim to find out what clothes she likes and why, what she fears with clothing, and the reasons she wears what she does. Ask questions. Don't judge her words. Listen carefully. Lis-ten for clues to who she might be trying to impress or gain the approval of. Hold your tongue even when you want to argue. And then give reflective advice. Be the person your daughter comes to in the morning to show her outfit to and the person she wants to go shopping with. Only then will you be able to speak into her life when it comes to modesty. Try saying things like:

- "I love the sense of style you've been developing. You have such eclectic taste. Have you seen this new web-site that sells vintage clothing? I really like some of the dresses they have."
- "Do you want to go to the mall on Saturday and see what the new spring lines are? We don't have to buy anything but it would be fun to look."
- "That's a really cute outfit. I wouldn't have ever thought to put that shirt with that skirt but it works."
- "Do you want my help packing for camp? I'd be happy to lay out a few outfits or wash a load of laundry."

- "What types of clothes do you think are most attractive on your body type? Why?"
- "I worry that shirt is a bit too low-cut. What do you think? Does it make you feel uncomfortable?"

2. Help Your Child Find Their Own Sense of Style
Pillar: Connection

I had a high school student come into my office the other day in tears because her parents weren't letting her buy the prom dress that she wanted. She showed me a picture of the dress and I immediately knew why the parents had intervened. The dress was black and short and had a deep V-neck that would have shown miles of décolletage.

I asked the girl what she liked about the dress and she said that she liked the black color and the fact that the fabric had little beads on it. She also liked the way the A-line shape looked on her. Together, we worked out a plan to talk to her mom about the types of dresses she liked and she went home that day and worked out a compromise with her parents. She bought a longer dress with a higher neckline that still had an A-line shape and beads. Win-win.

After years of working with kids, I realize that immodesty often isn't based on a girl's desire to be attractive or sexual, but instead in her desire to have control. Kids want to show the world who they are, that they are independent, creative, a growing person who has their own sense of style. And by helping our daughters to find their own sense of style—and to choose clothes that allow them to express themselves—we teach them how they can be stylish without being risqué. In doing so, they stop trying to grasp for control because they feel like they already have it. Try:

- Ask your daughter to tell you about the clothes she likes. Then work together to create a Pinterest board of outfits that you both like.
- Visit a store that has a stylist (try Nordstrom or Macy's) and ask the stylist to show your daughter which clothes look best on her body type.
- Don't nitpick her outfits, even if you think they look terrible. My youngest daughter often wore clashing stripes and plaid and I was mortified, but I bit my tongue as long as the articles were of appropriate length and fit.
- When you go shopping for clothes, let your daughter pick her own articles as long as they meet your modesty standards. And, yes, that means you let her buy the hot-pink leopard skirt even if it makes you crazy just looking at it.

3. Have as Few Rules as Possible
Pillar: Desire

I worked with the parents of two teenage boys who were really causing a lot of problems for their parents. Both boys seemed to want to push every house rule and to find ways to defy their parents at every turn. I pulled out a piece of paper and asked the parents to write down their list of house rules. I left the office, then came back five minutes later and read their list:

- 10 o'clock curfew.
- Make your bed before you go to school.
- Do all of your homework at your desk when you get home from school before you can watch TV, play with the iPad, or talk to friends.
- No cell phones or computers upstairs.
- You must participate in two extracurricular activities every year.

Now, this seemed like a very reasonable list of rules to me, but since the parents were having trouble with their sons being defiant and pressing the rules, I asked them how many of the rules were essential. At first they said all of them. But then we started talking.

"Why do you have a ten o'clock curfew?" I asked.

"Well, because kids have to have a curfew."

"Have your sons ever done anything to make you not trust them or to make you believe they can't stay out until, say, ten-thirty?" I asked.

"Well, no."

"So what if you take away the curfew altogether and tell them you'll make decisions based on each individual circumstance. On the week of a big test, you may require them to be in by nine. But at the start of summer, you may let them stay out until eleven. Take away the rule, and you give them a bit of control, without sacrificing your house standards."

The parents and I continued to go through the list of rules one by one. They decided to keep the rules that they had to make their beds each morning and that there were no computers or cell phones upstairs, as both of those things were important to the parents. But they decided it technically didn't matter if their sons had a bit of downtime before starting homework or if they did extracurricular activities.

The mom checked in with me a month later and said that getting rid of the rules was the best thing she had ever done. Her kids were much happier—they had more control and independence—and she wasn't always harping on them about things that simply didn't matter.

Modest dressing rules are another one of those things that can cause kids to revolt and do things like change their clothes in the bathroom at school or hide new purchases from parents.

And then it becomes not as much about immodesty as it does about control. In order to avoid this, my suggestion is to evaluate the rules you have. Keep the ones that you think are truly important and let the rest go. Try:

- Don't make rules like "skirts must be less than three inches above the knee" or you'll find yourself in a nit-picky battle of measuring and arguing. Just say "In our family, we dress modestly" and determine what that means on a case-by-case basis.
- Allow little concessions in order to avoid big ones. When she asks for a tattoo, buy a packet of metallic temporary tattoos and let her wear a gold armband. When she wants to dye her hair purple, pick up a pack of hair chalk and let her go to town.
- Allow different dress codes for different occasions. For example, require her to cover tank tops with a sweater for school, but if she's having an all-girl's pajama party at your house, let her wear that skimpy tank top on its own.
- Have a conversation about what standards would look like in context of 1 Timothy 2:9 that women should dress themselves in respectable apparel with modesty and self-control.

4. Never Make Modesty About Sex
Pillar: Growth

I had yet another conversation about modesty at our family pool. Once again, a group of first graders were swimming and a well-meaning mom complained to me that some of the girls were wearing bikinis. Now, I don't want to get into a debate about the merits (or demerits) of bikinis, but I did have to stop that mom and tell her that we couldn't be judging kids or other moms because of swim attire. The truth is, there is nothing sexual about a six-year-old wearing a bikini. If we start telling our daughters that they are being looked at by men based on their attire when they are six, I can only imagine what they will think when they are sixteen.

Now, I want to be very clear: I'm not saying that six-year-olds or sixteen-year-olds should be wearing skimpy bikinis. I allowed my daughters to wear very modest two-piece swimsuits and my granddaughters also have to wear suits that adequately cover. But I also don't even want to open the door to allowing my grandkids to think about things like sex and lust at such a young age. That's the mistake Jennifer made in the story I told earlier in this chapter: We can't tell them to dress modestly to keep from attracting men in a sexual way while at the same time talking to them about virtues like purity, chastity, and self-control. It doesn't jibe. We need to give reasons for modesty that connect with their age as well as your family's values. Say things like:

- "In our family, we believe that everyone should keep their bodies private. So we make sure girls wear one-piece suits and boys wear swim shirts."
- "I want you to be able to do all of your cool jumps and moves in the water without worrying about your suit falling off. Why don't we try one of these one-pieces?"
- "Your father and I have made a policy that our kids wear conservative bathing suits. We do this for a lot of reasons, one of them being that it keeps you safer from the sun, and another being that God calls us to be modest in the Bible."

FREE TO BE MODEST

Most of our kids probably aren't going to go for it if we try to get them to wear the things we want them to wear. (I learned this lesson when I suggested that my ten-year-old grandson wear a monogrammed initial sweater and a bow tie for his holiday pictures.) And let's face it: We probably don't want them to. Aside from the fact that monogrammed initial sweaters may be a teensy bit dorky, I want my kids to develop their own sense of style. And a heart to dress in a way that's respectful to boot.

The best thing we can do as parents and grandparents is teach our kids—both boys and girls—the value of modesty, how to treat the opposite gender with respect, and, yes, how to treat our bodies as temples of the most high.

Big concepts.

Good thing we have until monogrammed sweaters come back in style to pull it off.

———

Dear Jesus,

I want to lift up Erica and Emily as they start to work together to find modesty. Give Erica wise, loving words that allow Emily to draw closer to her mom and to find a middle ground between Emily's individual style and the biblical values that she needs to follow. Give Emily ears to hear and a heart that is willing to listen to her mom. Help Emily to develop an innate sense of modesty that allows her to grow into a strong woman of God.

Amen.

CHAPTER 13

Busting Up Bullying

(ERIN)

There is one whose rash words are like sword thrusts, but the tongue of the wise brings healing.

PROVERBS 12:18 (ESV)

I SAVED THIRTEEN DOLLARS ON those stupid blue shoes.

Thirteen dollars that I would have happily paid back to the store if they would have just warned me to put the sale shoes back on the rack and instead buy the solid black shoes that my son had asked for. But, no, I wanted to save money. I figured that blue shoes and black shoes were the same in the whole scheme of things. And I figured that my son who had never cared before about what he wore wouldn't care.

I figured wrong.

As soon as six-year-old Joey saw the shoes, he said, "Mom, those shoes are bright turquoise blue. I asked for black."

"Yeah, but blue and black are basically the same, right? And this is a really cool blue color!" I chirped, positive that Joey would be fine with the shoes.

And he was. For a day. "Fine, Mom, blue shoes are fine."

But the next day when I picked him up after school, he

leaped into the car and yanked his shoes off his feet. "I'll never wear these again," he cried. "Ever ever ever."

I'm a bit slow to catch on at times, and I had just spent the afternoon at the mall shopping for those blue shoes. He was certainly going to wear them again. "Of course you'll wear them again, silly," I replied with hardly a glance. "They are brand-new shoes and they are your only shoes that fit. You'll wear them every day for the rest of the school year."

Joey started to cry.

Because when I told him he was wearing those bright blue shoes every day for the rest of the school year, what he heard was far different from my words. He heard he was going to be made fun of every day for the rest of the school year. That he would be told he was wearing "girl's shoes" and that he was "weird" because his shoes weren't black. That he would be considered the weird kid, the outcast.

All because I was making him wear those stupid blue shoes.

I sat Joey down on the couch and asked him what had happened, and he told me that the kids were making fun of the shoes. That they had called him "Josephine" and were saying he should just go play with the girls if he was going to wear girly shoes.

Did I mention the shoes were blue?

Isn't blue a boy color?

Well, at the time I thought so.

But I learned something that day: In the world of first-grade politics, blue may be a boy's color, but turquoise is a girl's color. That, and kids are so, so mean. They find one little thing to pick on and they pick and they pick and they pick and they pick. Sweet boys and girls who just want to fit in and get along find themselves being bullied.

It's awful.

And it's a huge problem.

One that we as parents need to work together to stifle so that our kids can live in a world where they are safe to express themselves, to learn, to grow, to make friends, and to wear turquoise blue shoes. Let's see what Alex has to say about bullying:

Dear Erin,

My seven-year-old son A.J. is getting picked on at school by two boys. We'll call them James and John.

James and John are relentless! Last week they made fun of A.J. because he had a "baby lunchbox." This week they were taunting him about the new striped shirt that A.J. had picked out at the mall. He says he will never wear it again. And then today, A.J. came home from school with scraped knees. Apparently James and John had chased him on the playground telling him they were going to stick his head in the toilet. As A.J. ran away, he fell.

I'm about ready to head down to the school to do something about it. Maybe I should go sit by A.J. at lunch. I'm sure James and John wouldn't dare pick on him if I was there. I just can't stand to watch my son be picked on like this and for the bullies to just get away with it day after day. What should I do?

Alexander

I always assumed that social issues would spring up when my kids reached middle school and before that, it would be all tea parties and Lego towers. But I was wrong! Joey's shoe incident happened in first grade. First grade. I've since learned that kids who have a tendency to bully start being bullies at a very young age. And sweet, tenderhearted kids who just want to please pay the consequences.

Alexander,

I hate this for A.J. I can't imagine how he must feel going to school and feeling scared that he's going to be picked on. He must feel so alone and afraid. James and John sound like they are really nasty bullies!

I totally relate to you wanting to head down to the school and do something about it. I would, too, but I want to warn you: That might just make things worse for A.J. When a parent or teacher intervenes in a dramatic way—such as you going down to the school and sitting with A.J. at lunch—bullies often grow more intense. Instead, we have to teach A.J. how to handle the bullies in a way that will keep them quiet for good.

I have a few ideas.

Erin

BIG PICTURE THEMES

- Friendship
- Empathy
- Kindness
- Bullying
- Understanding
- Social engineering

DISCIPLESHIP FOR KIDS WHO ARE DEALING WITH BULLYING

But I say to you, love your enemies and pray for those who persecute you.

MATTHEW 5:44 (ESV)

I'm going to point out the obvious here: In every bullying situation there is a kid being bullied. And there is also a bully.

There's an A.J. And there's also a John and a James. Many of us will parent A.J.s—we will navigate the tears, the fear, the not knowing what to do. But many of us will also parent Johns and Jameses. And we will also navigate tears (our own) and fear (what is my kid doing) and not knowing what to do.

I've parented both.

Yes, that's right. Just last year, I got a call from my son Will's pre-K teacher.

Mrs. Cafitz explained to me that another little boy in the class—Charlie—was coming to school crying every morning. Charlie had told his mom that Will was hitting him and he was afraid to go to school because of it. Charlie's mom—who is a teacher herself—had called the teacher and asked if she could get to the bottom of it.

Will's teacher had assured her she would. She carefully watched Will and Charlie all day and never saw any problems. They sat next to each other but Will never seemed to hurt Charlie and often the two of them talked together. At the end of the day, Will's teacher pulled Will aside and asked if he had ever hit Charlie and Will responded with big, wide eyes that he had never.

Will's teacher had believed him.

So she was calling me to tell me about what had gone on and to let me know that she was going to talk to Charlie's mom as well but she was confident that Will hadn't done anything wrong and that Charlie was blaming his fear of school on innocent little Will.

I should have heard those words and known better.

I pulled Will aside that night and asked him if anything strange was going on at school. Will's eyes grew wide and then narrowed. "He told Mrs. Cafitz? I told him not to!"

"Who are you talking about, Will?"

"Charlie!" he snarled.

I pressed further. "What do you think Charlie said?"

"Well, that I'm hitting him!"

I closed my eyes, praying it wasn't true. "Are you hitting him, Will?"

"Well, yeah. I just wait until Mrs. Cafitz turns her head and hit him on the arm. Then I smile and tell Charlie not to tell. He never does."

I am not sure I have ever been so mortified in my entire life.

I immediately called Mrs. Cafitz and then Charlie's mom. I explained what I had learned and we met the next day. We talked about what bullying meant, and Mrs. Cafitz told Will that he was going to have to sit at a table on his own away from Charlie. Additionally, Will was going to have to be supervised on the playground and in class so he didn't hit Charlie again. Will did apologize.

Several months later, Will and Charlie developed a sweet little friendship. I'm pretty sure the incident is forgotten by both of them.

I'm not making light of this—Will's actions were unacceptable. He was being a bully and poor Charlie was being bullied. I don't want to gloss over that fact or belittle it. Thank Jesus we caught it before someone got hurt too badly and that Charlie and his mom were willing to forgive and move on. We have had many family conversations about this issue and talked a lot about kindness and empathy and grace. I pray daily that Will can resist the temptation to bully again.

Because bullying is serious.

While I don't want my kids to be bullied, I desperately don't want my kids to be bullies.

I'm telling you this story not because I just love reliving one of the more embarrassing incidents in my parenting tenure, but because I want to make it clear that some of us—yes, even those of us who raise our kids in Sunday school and teach our kids that hitting is never nice and pray daily that our kids will be kind— will have kids who choose to bully. And so when we disciple our kids on this issue, we have to disciple them from both sides.

DISCIPLESHIP FOR KIDS WHO ARE BEING BULLIED

- **Talk about the bullying without absolutes.** Your child may feel like his *entire* social life is over and like he'll *never* have friends again. He may say that *everyone* feels the same as the bully. And that *every* word the bully says is probably true. These are real feelings! Being bullied can be devastating for a kid. But being bullied does not mean your kid's social life is over and it certainly doesn't mean that he will be bullied for his entire life. In Psalm 37, David, who was being bullied by Saul, wrote: "Fret not yourself because of evildoers; be not envious of wrongdoers! For they will soon fade like the grass and wither like the green herb. Trust in the LORD, and do good; dwell in the land and befriend faithfulness. Delight yourself in the LORD, and he will give you the desires of your heart." As we befriend faithfulness, God will come beside us and give us the desires of our heart. Now that's an absolute I can get behind.
- **Try repaying evil with kindness.** I think everyone knows that the Bible tells us to do good to those who hate us (it's in Luke 6:28, if you want to read it yourself), but when a child is being picked on, this is such a hard prerogative to follow. But you can do it! Sit down with

your kid and ask him how he could do good for the kid who is bullying him. This probably won't mean drawing him a picture or inviting him to Sunday school—at least not yet—but you could pray for him together. You could say hello when you saw him in the schoolyard. You could smile at him when you really want to scream. Even little kindnesses can make a big difference to a bully who is likely struggling with his own issues of acceptance and anger.

- **Seek Him first thing in the morning.** Again, I don't want to make light of bullying, as I realize it's a serious issue that needs to be addressed. So the last thing I want to do is throw out some trite "just ignore it" advice and cause your child to feel more isolated and alone. But in Matthew 6:33, we are told to "seek first the Kingdom of God and His righteousness." Then all of the other stuff will be added to that. So before school or church or playgroup each day when you worry that your child may get bullied, start your day by seeking Him and His righteousness. Wake him up a bit early and sit together and pray for righteousness and wisdom and grace. Discuss what it means to be righteous and to honor God with our actions. And let him start his day seeking Jesus and let all of the other stuff fall into place.

DISCIPLESHIP FOR KIDS WHO ARE BEING BULLIES

- **Set a vision for who your child is and what he stands for.** Remind your child that your family lives by Galatians 5:22, applying the fruits of the spirit such as love, joy, peace, patience, kindness, goodness, faith-fulness, gentleness, and self-control into every area of your lives. This is the standard that you have for behav-ior and the treatment of others, and bullying breaks that standard.

- **Pick a fruit of the week.** Choose one of the fruits of the spirit each week for nine weeks. Work together to come up with specific ways you can apply that fruit of the spirit to your lives that week. For example, on love week, you can write nice notes to teachers and friends or volunteer at a soup kitchen. On joy week, you could write a list of all the things that bring joy to the world or sing joyful songs to God. On peace week, talk about conflict resolution and how to be at peace with all men.

- **Ask your child what exactly is going on.** When I asked Will why he was hitting Charlie, he just shrugged and said, "Charlie is just so funny when I hit him. He makes a scowl face." Cue bad mom anger welling up inside of me. When Will said that, I pulled out the Bible and read James 4:2: "You desire and do not have, so you murder. You covet and cannot obtain, so you fight and quarrel. You do not have, because you do not ask." I explained to him that God says that sometimes when we have confusing feelings—envy, greed, anger, desire—we respond by being mean. But that's never what a God-seeking kid does. Instead, we press into the Lord for our comfort and He will give us the desires of our heart.

- **Clothe yourselves with kindness.** Colossians 3:12 tells us to put kindness on like it's a T-shirt or a pair of jeans. I explained that metaphor to Will after he had bul-lied Charlie and we talked about how kindness should be the first thing they see when they see us and the last thing they see when we walk away. From there, we made kindness the positive focus of our questions. When I picked him up from school, I asked, "What is one kind thing you did today?" and when he went to a play date, I asked, "What is one kind thing your friend did at his house?" We told him how to clothe himself in kindness in his classroom so even when the teacher wasn't looking, kindness would show through his actions.

PRACTICAL SOLUTIONS FOR KIDS WHO ARE DEALING WITH BULLYING

For God gave us a spirit not of fear but of power and love and self-control.

2 TIMOTHY 1:7 (ESV)

There was a girl who picked on me when I was in elementary school.

She was taller than me, prettier than me (or so I thought), and a better basketball player than me, which meant a whole lot in Central Oregon where the snow kept us inside all winter long, making it the only sport. She made sure I knew it pretty much every day on the playground. She would push me off the swing set and say, "There's no room for you here," or she would set up a recess basketball game and tell everyone that I wasn't good enough to play. I remember after one particular incident, I burst into tears and sat at the edge of the playground sobbing for the rest of recess.

I glanced up at one point and saw her staring at me and laughing.

I was devastated.

That night, I sobbed to my mom, explaining that I was destined to never have friends because *everyone* loved the girl who was bullying me and *nobody* wanted to play with me. I told her I would *never* go to school again and that I would probably *never* speak to anyone my age ever again. (Do you remember what I said about absolutes?)

I'm sure my mom's heart was completely wrenching inside, that she was biting her lip and holding back the urge to call that recess monitor up and tell her what she thought of me being excluded. But my mom didn't explode.

Instead, she gave me some tricks that would help me to stop bullying in its tracks.

1. Teach Your Kid About the Flat Face
Pillar: Growth

That day after school, my mom taught me about the flat face. She explained to me that bullies want a reaction. They want to see someone fly off the handle or start crying or to scream back. They want to hurt someone else so they can ease their own pain. And so the best thing you can do to stop them is to not give that reaction.

My mom had me practice it in the mirror.

I forced myself to remove all emotion from my face—no happiness, no sadness, no anger, no tears—and instead, just put on a flat, emotionless expression. My mom then taught me to say with a dull voice, "I don't care about that anyway." My mom told me that no matter how much I cared—no matter how upset I was or how angry I was, I couldn't show that emotion to the bully.

She also made me a promise that if I kept that flat face on for the bully, I could be as angry or sad or despondent as I wanted once I got home. It was important for me to find a safe adult to share my emotions and feelings with about the situation—just not in front of the bully.

After practicing, I tried it the next day.

The girl excluded me from a four-square game, but that day, instead of crying, I shrugged and said, "I don't want to play four square anyway." And then I walked away. Now, inside, I was weeping from loneliness and desperate to play that game, but I stuck to my mom's game plan.

And it worked!

The next day, my bully excluded me again, but after the third day of flat face, the bullying fizzled out. And she got to a place where she just sort of ignored me. She wasn't my best friend, but she certainly wasn't picking on me every day.

This strategy works great for minor bullying—I'm not talking about bullying where your kid is in physical or emotional danger (in which case you should seek professional help) but the day-to-day taunting and meanness that wears at kids.

It works, because it takes the emotional power away from the bully and puts it in the hands of the victim.

And it shows the bully that whatever he says, he doesn't have the power to destroy your kid's heart.

2. Teach Your Kid Not to Believe Words
Pillar: Growth

Your kid is not too stupid or too wimpy or too slow or too fast or too skinny or too athletic or too anything. Your kid is a child of God, created by our King to do great works. There is nothing that a bully can say that will change that. But that doesn't mean those words don't hurt. Because I think we all know from experience that words really can hurt.

Take a glass of water and fill it up in the sink. Tell your child to pretend that the water is negative words and the cup is their soul. Then turn the cup upside down and let the water pour off the bottom. Tell your child that the best way to keep those negative words from hurting is to turn over their cup. To allow the negative words to spill out and never to enter their heart or soul for even a moment.

Similar to the flat face, the best way to do this is to teach your kid to look at the bully and say, "That's not true," and then walk away. Tell your kid that she doesn't have to listen to the words. She can simply turn away or turn her attention elsewhere. Sing a song in her head. Talk to another friend. But turn that glass upside down so the words can't get inside.

3. Take Your Kids' Words Seriously...but Don't Intervene
Pillar: Connection

Your kid needs to know that he has a safe place to go to when he is being bullied. He needs a shoulder to cry on, a listening ear to talk to, someone to hold him up, someone who believes in him. So when your kid comes to you about being bullied, take it seriously. Immediately stop what you are doing and listen. Ask questions. Support him. Give him ideas on how to make it stop. If it continues, consider going to a teacher or the school for help. Make sure your kid knows that you are on his side and you are there to protect him.

There is a huge caveat: It often makes bullying worse if you intervene in a vocal way. My mom tells the story of a mom who decided to stop a bully by coming to the playground to have a chat with the boy who was bullying. And it worked— for a day. No one bullied her son while she was there. But the next day? The bullies were not only back at it, but they also had fresh fodder for the fire: They now bullied him about having to have his mom help him.

The general rule of thumb is to let your child or the

authorities that be (such as teachers or principals) be the ones who interact with the bully. As for you, you interact with your child. Give him the tools he needs to stand tall and the support he needs to know he is loved.

4. Don't Necessarily Believe Everything Your Kid Says
Pillar: Desire

Remember that story I told you about my son Will hitting his sweet friend Charlie in class? Will's innocent "I would *never* hit Charlie" fooled both me and his teacher. For a while, all of us started thinking that maybe Charlie was making it up. Kids can be very convincing. And conniving. This taught me very quickly that (a) I should never believe everything my kid says and (b) I need to ask lots of questions when I hear things that may or may not have happened at school.

This can go both ways.

A friend of mine had a daughter who came home from school every day crying that three boys were picking on her. She told her mom that the boys chased her and threw sand at her and grabbed her clothes and pulled on them at recess. Her mom had been furious and had called the school to ask the teacher to observe them on the playground the next day. The teacher watched and it turned out to be just the opposite: The little girl was chasing the boys and grabbing their clothes and throwing sand on them. And, worst of all, she was telling them that if they told anyone, she would just tell the teachers they were the bullies. My friend was mortified.

There is a fine line that we have to walk between believing and supporting our kids when they tell us how they are feeling and trusting every word they say. My advice to you is simple: Ask lots of questions. Kids aren't that sophisticated. They aren't that great of liars. And the more you dig, the more truth will be revealed.

Once you know the truth, you will be able to support your kid so that he isn't bullied. And so that he isn't a bully.

HELPING OUR KIDS DEAL WITH BULLYING

Bullying is a big issue in schools today—and it's something that we as parents must take very seriously. If you hear stories from your kids or about your kids that sound like bullying, believe them and do something about them. Call for help. Get the school involved. Talk to your child. Disciple your child so that you can make sure that God's love and kindness replace the pain of bullying in the life of your child.

Father God,

You are the great comforter. You come beside those who are bullied, those who feel lonely and isolated and unworthy and You lift them up. So come beside A.J. and his father and fill them with Your peace. Help them to resist the temptation to feel down or despondent and instead, to get their peace and hope from You. Amen.

──── CHAPTER 14 ────

Flee from Sexual Immorality

(ELLEN)

Do not be conformed to this world, but be transformed by the renewal of your mind, that by testing you may discern what is the will of God, what is good and acceptable and perfect.

ROMANS 12:2 (ESV)

I HAD ALWAYS ADMIRED SANDY.

I had read two of her books about faith and family and heard her on the radio, so when I heard she was coming into town to speak at a women's conference, I bought a ticket. Afterward, I went over to meet her. She told me about her newest book and I shared about mine, we talked about our backgrounds in education and school leadership, and I even showed her pictures of my grandkids. We hit it off! I was thrilled when she asked me to head down to Starbucks after the event to get a cup of coffee.

When we sat down with our hazelnut lattes, I looked at the woman who had mentored me through her words for so long and saw a face that was crestfallen. Where had her joy and enthusiasm gone? Suddenly, before I even had the chance to take a sip of coffee, the tears started to fall and her story came tumbling out.

"I have no idea how I even got through that talk," she moaned. Between sobs, she shared how earlier that week she had learned that her only daughter, Hayley, who was wrapping up her senior year in high school, was pregnant. Just months before, she had been accepted to a prestigious college, where she planned to join her older brother. She had won a volleyball scholarship!

Everything had been perfect for Hayley until she had met Robbie on Instagram.

But now, instead of heading off to college, Hayley planned to move into an apartment with her boyfriend, Robbie. She had told her parents that it was only right that they would be raising this child together. And she needed to get out from under their umbrella anyway.

Sandy continued to sob.

"I have always carefully monitored her activities. I have no idea how this could have happened! How did I allow my daughter to become sexually active? I feel like such a failure as a mom!" But then came the kicker: "I guess the first thing I need to do is cancel my speaking tour and my next book release. It's not like I can mentor families now when I've so clearly failed as a mom."

I moved my chair over by her and put my arm around her and we sat there for twenty minutes crying together. Even though I hear similar stories on a regular basis, my heart breaks every time.

Feeling like failures.

Wondering what they did wrong.

The answer is they've done nothing wrong and everything wrong. We are all humans who have made mistakes raising our kids. Likewise, our kids are all human who make decisions in isolation of their parents. And our values.

Sexual sin is pervasive in a culture that entices our kids to conform to it. And some kids fall into that trap. What can we do preventatively as parents? How should we respond when our kids fail?

These are the kinds of questions I often get from parents. Here's an e-mail I received this spring from a parent of an eighth grader.

> *Dear Ellen,*
>
> *I don't know what to do.*
>
> *My thirteen-year-old daughter Marissa is "going out" with a guy in her class. I overheard her telling her best friend that they had "French kissed" after school. I don't even know what she meant by "French kiss" but I do know that I don't like it.*
>
> *My husband thinks we should tell her that she isn't old enough to date and tell her she is forbidden from seeing this guy. But I'm afraid that will make her so mad at us. Not to mention, she sees him every day at school, so we can't exactly keep her away from him.*
>
> *What should we do?*
>
> *Terri*

A thirteen-year-old French kissing? A seventeen-year-old pregnant? How is it that these young kids—kids who grow up in Christian homes and with Christian values—are being exposed to sexuality at such a young age? How can we protect our kids in a way that instills a desire to do right? These are the questions that parents are asking, and to be honest, I'm glad. It's good that parents are concerned, that we're having these conversations. Because together, we can help our kids to build the foundation for healthy marriages and relationships as they grow older. Here's how I answered Terri:

> *Dear Terri,*
>
> *I think some of the most stressful and confusing issues that come up with parents involve their kids getting into romantic relationships. And I can see why! We live in a sex-crazed*

culture where kids are given confusing messages about love and sex. In our society, Christian values like purity and modesty are often dismissed because they are "old-fashioned" or "stifling," yet the emotional, physical, and spiritual risks of sexual immorality are so frightening that they can't be ignored.

What should we as parents do?

One important thing: Do not forbid Marissa from seeing her boyfriend. This will likely make her want to pursue him more and, worse, will cause her to believe she has to hide it from you. Instead, this is a time for you to help Marissa understand God's vision for relationships and sex in a way that's God-honoring and that will help her to desire purity, modesty, morality, and all of the things that God hopes for our relationships. I have a few ideas for you.

Sincerely,
Ellen

BIG PICTURE THEMES

- Purity
- Promiscuity
- Sexual sin
- Sexuality
- Teen pregnancy
- Modesty
- Virtue

DISCIPLESHIP IN THE AREA OF SEXUAL SIN

In the letter that Terri wrote to me, she said her husband wanted to forbid her daughter from seeing her boyfriend. Likewise, I hear from parents all the time who say things like "Our kids aren't allowed to date until they are sixteen" or "Our kids will be courting, not dating." I want to caution you against this.

Here's why: There is no biblical mandate that says, "Thou shalt not date until you are sixteen years old." And there is no biblical mandate for courting or having a chaperone on a date or not attending the school dance when you are in middle school. These are rules that many parents make, but I would venture that oftentimes they do more harm than good. Why? Because they put regulations around something that should be a desire of the heart.

In 1 Corinthians 6:18, we are told to "flee from sexual immorality." The Bible is very clear that sex is for the marriage bed.

When our kids are seeking God's will for their lives, working toward sanctification and seeking righteousness, they will desire to follow that command.

Not because their parents told them they would be grounded if they didn't. But because they truly desire to do what is right by God. They are following the commands of Matthew 6:33 and seeking His kingdom first.

If this heart desire to follow God is the ultimate goal, then rules like "you can't date until you're sixteen" undermine that goal. Who is to say your child will have that true heart desire to follow God when she is sixteen? Who is to say she won't have it when she is fifteen? By setting a bunch of rules around dating, you are basically giving your child permission to follow your rules instead of seeking God's.

Likewise, rules about sexuality often lead to less conversation and communication. In the example of Marissa, the eighth grader who had "French kissed" her boyfriend, her mom, Terri, admitted that she had no idea what Marissa meant by "French kiss." They had never talked about it. So the first step for someone like Terri would be not to ban her daughter from French kissing, but instead to talk to her daughter about French kissing, about what it meant to her, about values and sexual immorality.

Maybe her daughter was calling "French kissing" a peck on the cheek. (Don't laugh: I had a sweet sixth-grade girl in my office who said the same thing just this week.) Maybe she meant hugging while kissing (another misconception kids have had). Or maybe she actually was French kissing him, in which case the conversation is even more important.

Either way, making a rule about "no French kissing" without conversation would likely do nothing to stop Marissa from French kissing and instead cause her to get angry with her parents.

What if you were to replace the rules with conversation? With open communication, with prayerful consideration, with Bible study? What if your family limits were created based on mutual understanding and conviction, instead of on arbitrary rules that you threw out there? What if this turned into a long-term, connection-building conversation between you and your kids? Here are a few things you could talk about:

- **We are free in Christ.** Galatians 5:13 describes the freedom that comes from being in an intimate relationship with Jesus. "For you were called to freedom, brothers. Only do not use your freedom as an opportunity for the flesh, but through love serve one another." So many teenagers start to believe that freedom means they should seek their own happiness or do what feels right. But God wants a much-more-free freedom for us. He wants us to truly be free and to use that freedom not to fulfill our own desires, but to serve Him and others.
- **We have the power to guard our hearts and bodies.** In Psalm 119:133, David begs God to "keep steady

[his] steps according to [His] promise, and let no iniquity get dominion over [him]." In Psalm 119:9 we are told that we can stay pure by guarding our hearts according to His word. Through intentional prayer and with his help, we can do what's right unto the Lord.

- **Sexual sin is different from other sin.** Have a discussion about 1 Corinthians 6:18–20. Why does God distinguish sexual sin from other kinds of sin? "Flee from sexual immorality. Every other sin a person commits is outside the body, but the sexually immoral person sins against his own body. Or do you not know that your body is a temple of the Holy Spirit within you, whom you have from God? You are not your own, for you were bought with a price. So glorify God in your body."

- **What is God's desire for us in regards to sex?** With your teens, do a study together on the Song of Solomon, a ballad about a man and woman preparing and looking forward to marriage. The Song of Solomon provides a biblical account of the beauty of human sexuality and marriage. In the Song of Solomon, we see a glimpse of redeemed sexuality, that God created physical intimacy for permanent relationships, ones that are also spiritually and emotionally intimate.

PRACTICAL SOLUTIONS TO AVOID SEXUAL SIN

Poor Sandy!

She had such high hopes for her daughter—and every single thing about her life was changed in one moment of weakness. It was a devastating blow, but as I sat there in Starbucks holding Sandy's hand, I reminded her that God wasn't finished with their family yet. All have sinned and fallen short of the glory of God. And God uses us in our weakness just as he uses us in His strength.

Sandy's life and her ministry were not over.

And neither was her daughter's.

That said, every parent has to ask themselves two questions: First, what can they do to help their kids avoid the temptation of sexual sin? Second, what can they do to help their kids pick up the pieces that have already fallen? I have a few ideas for both situations below.

1. Help Your Kids Set Their Own Limits
Pillar: Desire

By the time our youngest daughter, Alisa, was in high school, we had gotten wiser in our approach to teaching about sexuality and limits. With our older two kids, we had tried the "rules" approach—no dating until they were fifteen—and while neither of them fell into major sexual sin, we had few conversations about the issue. We just didn't talk about it, which meant we never really connected with their hearts.

With Alisa, we learned from our past experiences. Instead of focusing on what she shouldn't do and teaching her to view her sexuality negatively, we worked to maintain an open dialogue with her and talk about God's perfect plan for her future in marriage. I remember so many sweet discussions with her and helping guide her in the process she went through to establish her own boundaries and limits.

Yes, we let her establish her own boundaries and limits.

Not in a "do whatever you want to do" sort of way, but instead in a "let's talk about this and have a conversation and come up with a plan together" sort of way. If your child doesn't think she is ready to date, then support her in that and hold to that rule. If she feels like she is ready and can trust the guy who asks her out (and if you trust him too), then let her.

In addition to limits about sexuality and dating, work with your kids to come up with family guidelines around the use of media. After the "hot cheerleader incident" that we talked about in the introduction of this book, my daughter and my grandkids worked together to come up with a set of rules for using devices. Together, they came up with the rule that they aren't allowed to bring unprotected devices upstairs or to their rooms, they aren't allowed to go to houses where Internet or cell phone use is unsupervised, and they aren't allowed to play games that may have ads for other more explicit games. My daughter also has kids who come over with phones or iPads "check in" their devices to her before the kids go outside or upstairs to play. These seem like very strict rules—and they are—but I am convinced that media is an area where parents must be very vigilant due to explicit sexual material that is so readily available.

Interestingly, since Joey and Kate helped come up with these guidelines based on their own experiences, they readily abide by them. I've found that kids are much more likely to uphold limits that they set themselves and are much more likely to discuss them with you as they learn and grow if you have started the dialogue.

Now, I feel like I need to address the question that is probably niggling at the back of many of your minds: How far is too far? I hear that question at least once a week—mostly from teenagers who I mentor, but also from their parents. And the answer is always very vague. The Bible says to flee from sexual immorality (1 Corinthians 6:18), and it also clearly states that sex outside of marriage is sexual sin. That is pretty clear. But there is quite a bit of ambiguity on questions like how old a kid should be to date, courting versus dating, going to dances, kissing, and hand-holding and the like. I don't think this was a mistake or exclusion on God's part, but instead an understanding that each person and family is different.

We have families at our school who have shared values that kissing is okay as long as both kids have talked about their values on sex and desire to uphold them. We have other families that don't allow their kids to go on unsupervised dates until they are married. These are family values that these families have come up with. I want to encourage you to prayerfully come up with values that your family can hold to, without worrying about what others are doing or saying. Have conversations. Follow the biblical mandate to flee from sexual immorality. Help your kids to understand what righteousness is. Then come up with guidelines that work within that framework.

2. Talk About Sex with Your Kids
Pillar: *Growth*

I know: The idea of talking to your kids about sex makes you a bit weak in the knees. If you are one of those parents who would rather, say, scrub peanut butter off the underside of your cabinets than talk to your kids about sex, then you are not alone. But that doesn't mean you shouldn't do it.

Think of it this way: If you are their primary and most trusted source of information about sexuality, then you are naturally the person they will come to when they have questions. And would you want them to come to you instead of, say, Henry's tenth-grade brother who lives down the street? The thought makes you shudder, doesn't it? So swallow that fear. Talk to them with confidence and love. Show them that sex is never something to be ashamed of or embarrassed of, but instead, something to be honored and treasured as one of God's biggest gifts for marriage. Here are some ways you can start the conversation, even with kids as young as five or six:

Younger kids:

- Start early by painting a positive picture of God's design for sex and marriage. Properly refer to body parts and their functions. Be their "expert." Answer questions honestly in age-appropriate ways and be their unfailing source of good, solid information.
- Teach boundaries for young children. Explain that their private parts are private and shouldn't be touched. Explain the difference between good touches and bad touches. Tell her that it's okay to say no when she feels uncomfortable.

As they reach middle school:

- Educate and inform your kids about pornography. It seems uncomfortable, but a study at the University of New Hampshire* showed that 42 percent of kids ages ten to fourteen have seen pornography and that the average first exposure was at the age of nine. Yikes. Talk to your kids about what pornography is and how it hurts both boys and girls.

---

* Janis Wolak, Kimberly Mitchell, and David Finkelhor, "Unwanted and Wanted Exposure to Online Pornography in a National Sample of Youth Internet Users," *Pediatrics* 119, no. 2 (February 2007).

- Give your kids words to say when they find themselves in a situation that makes them uncomfortable. Many kids think they need an eloquent speech about what is right and what is wrong for every situation. Remind your kids that the most important thing is to get themselves away from a potential problem. They can always circle back for a more detailed conversation if they want to talk more. But in the moment, it's perfectly acceptable to say, "I'm not feeling well. I'm heading home!" or "My mom needs me home, so I'm leaving."
- Talk about what makes a person beautiful. Girls are under considerable pressure to look hot. They dress seductively because they try to find their identity and influence in their bodies. Likewise, boys are under pressure to look for "hot chicks" and to focus on a girl's outward appearance instead of what's inside. So spend time talking about what beauty really means to God.

Teens:

- Work together to come up with guidelines for social situations. Talk about the types of situations that could potentially cause problems (i.e., a one-on-one date or time alone in their bedroom with a friend and a computer) and then talk about how those situations can be avoided. Come up with alternatives that allow your teen to have a social life and allow her to develop healthy relationships with the opposite sex without putting herself in a risky situation. For example, host a movie night or game night or dinner for eight in your house.
- Talk about how kids can protect themselves against abuse, sex trafficking, predators, date rape, and "going

too far" in a moment of weakness. These are tough conversations, ones that kids will likely moan at when you
bring them up, but it is so important for your kids to
know how to handle tough situations and more importantly, for them to know that they can come to you no
matter what has happened for help. Let them know you
will be their sounding board, their 10:00 p.m. ride home,
their *anything*, if they just talk to you.

• There's a lot of pressure in the teen world. Girls are pressured to do things sexually that they are uncomfortable with. Boys are pressured to do things sexually that
they are uncomfortable with. Both genders are made to
feel "lame" or "prude" if they hold to high standards of
morality. And both genders are made to feel awkward in
relationships with the opposite gender due to the rules,
regulations, pressures, and hype about sexuality. There's
a whole lot of pressure out there. So talk to your teen
about what he or she is feeling pressured about and dialogue about how they can maintain their desire to do
right in spite of that pressure.

3. Remember That God's Mercies Are New Every Morning
Pillar: Growth

Sandy told me that her daughter—who had once had a prom-
ising future—had ruined her entire life by getting pregnant.
She sobbed that her daughter would never go to college, would
never get married, would never have a future. But that's just
not true. In Lamentations 3:22–23, we read that God's mercies
never come to an end and that they are new every morning.
Emphasis mine. He will never forsake us. Never abandon us.
Never give up the great plan He has for us.

Which means that while Sandy's daughter may have a few bumps in the road, her life is not over. Who knows what God has in store for her? Maybe it's a wonderful teen pregnancy ministry. Maybe it's college in a few years. Maybe God wants her to marry her boyfriend and will allow Sandy's family to bring him to the Lord. Who knows? But I do know that God has not abandoned Sandy's daughter due to her mistake. And God has not wavered in his undeniable, unchangeable love.

When dealing with your kids after they have made a big mistake, I think the main thing we have to do is get rid of the concept of "damaged goods." Psalm 103:12–13 says, "As far as the east is from the west, so far does he remove our transgressions from us. As a father shows compassion to his children, so the Lord shows compassion to those who fear Him." At any point Sandy's daughter can seek a pure heart. She can be forgiven and start new. They will need to work through the consequences of their choices, but God is a God of redemption and renewal.

Innocence is about never having experienced evil. Purity is about knowing what it is and learning to not partake even when faced with the temptation of doing so. Romans 13:14 says, "Put on the Lord Jesus Christ and make no provision for the flesh to gratify its desires." Sandy has to stand by her daughter and make sure she knows that regardless of her sinful nature and the mistakes she makes, she is loved and accepted by Jesus. He is her hope. His kindness moves her to change.

Romans 6:20–22 says that "for when you were slaves of sin, you were free in regard to righteousness. But what fruit were you getting at the time from things of which you are now ashamed? For the end of those things is death. But now you have been set free from sin and have become slaves of God, the fruit that you get leads to sanctification and its end, eternal life." There is so much deep, abiding, everlasting hope in that verse.

So when your kids have failed—in a big way—don't condemn them or judge them. Stand with them. Forgive. Help them to move on. And allow Jesus's undeniable love to wash them clean.

4. Don't Let Your Kids' Choices Change Your Life
Pillar: Connection

As Sandy cried on my shoulder that day in Starbucks, she said over and over that she had to quit her ministry, that she wouldn't be able to write her next book or continue her speaking tour. I looked her in the eye and told her very seriously that those words were hogwash.

There's much we can, and must do, as parents to influence our kids. But we are not ultimately responsible for their choices and decisions. When a child's life is seriously altered by poor decisions, it's devastating for a parent. Adding a heavy—and unnecessary—burden of guilt makes it impossible to bear.

One thing I know for sure is that no one has parented perfectly. No one. When I look back and think about all the things I wish I had handled differently, it gets me nowhere but discouraged. But when I realize that Jesus became real to me through my failures and mistakes, I know that it will be the same for my children, who He loves more than I do.

So when your children have sinned—when they make a mistake, especially a life-altering mistake—you can be upset. Angry even. But don't let it alter who you are or what you stand for. Walk forward confidently and make the best decisions you can from that day forward. Connect with your child.

Love them. Help them. Pray for them. But don't rehash the things you should have done or should have said.

God has forgiven you.

He has forgiven your child.

Now walk forward in hope.

FLEEING SEXUAL IMMORALITY

I am going to make an assertion that may make some of you uncomfortable, but I'll say it anyway: Your child will face sexual temptation in his or her childhood. It's everywhere. In every private school, public school, Sunday school, library, church, home, sports team, and movie. You will not be able to protect your kid from knowing about sex and from having to make decisions about sex.

So equip your kids to handle it.

Give your kids the tools they need to not only understand God's design for sex and sexuality, but also how to handle any situation they may face when it comes to sex. Teach them the difference between innocence and purity and restoration. Disciple them, talk to them, connect with them so that they can develop hearts that truly desire Him and develop minds that are able to make decisions that lead to strong, healthy families that serve Him.

———

Heavenly Father,

Please be with Sandy and her daughter. Fill them with Your mercy and help them to navigate this new situation with love and grace. And be with the precious child that is growing in

Sandy's daughter. We know that no child is a mistake and that You have big plans for this beautiful child. Likewise, be with Terri and Marissa as they navigate tough conversations about sex and limits. Help them to be wise, understanding, and most of all, to seek you first. Amen.

——— **CHAPTER 15** ———

Fear Not

(ERIN)

The fear of man lays a snare, but whoever trusts in the Lord is safe.

PROVERBS 29:25 (ESV)

WE WERE ON FAMILY VACATION staying on the fifth floor of a hotel.

After a long day of white-water rafting, we walked into our hotel room and set down our wet towels and slipped off our still-soaked water shoes. Just as I turned on the shower for five-year-old Will to get in, the fire alarm started to beep.

Will took off.

Before I even realized what was going on, he darted out of the room and sprinted down the hall and into the stairwell. I raced after him down the stairs, listening to the echoes of his tiny feet below me as I desperately tried to keep up. I burst out the door to see my five-year-old sprinting across the busy parking lot in his swim trunks, not even pausing to look for cars.

I sent my ten-year-old after him (he can run faster than me) and told him to grab and hold on to him until I caught up.

When I finally caught up (huffing and puffing), I grabbed

Will and stooped down. His eyes frantically jumped from me to the building. "What happened, buddy?"

He shivered. "There was a loud, loud noise. I had to get out!"

"But, buddy, we have talked about this. That beeping was a fire alarm. Remember when we watched that video about firefighters? When there is a fire alarm, we walk out of the building and don't run. Running like that could have made it so you fell down the stairs or hurt yourself. Or you could have gotten hit by a car. When we hear a fire alarm, we calmly get outside as quickly as we can without panicking."

He nodded at me and said he understood.

He told me he would remember that for next time.

He really seemed like he got it.

Which is why I was so confused when it happened again an hour later.

Apparently our motel was having issues with their fire alarm system, because after we got the all-clear to go back to our room and went back upstairs once again to change and shower, the fire alarm went off yet a second time.

Can you guess what Will did?

Yep. The kid panicked. He ran down those stairs a second time. He ran across that parking lot a second time. He did exactly the opposite of what I had told him to do.

Was he being rebellious? Disobedient? I don't think so. Instead, I think he was so overcome by fear that he just didn't know how to handle himself. And because of that, he put himself in an even more dangerous situation.

Many kids have fears. And kids like Will often let those fears drive their behavior—and not always in good ways. For example, read this letter I got from a dad named Mike:

Dear Erin,

My daughter Nora is scared of cats.

Not lions, mind you, but cats. Like the little tiny fluffy white kitten that basks in the sunshine in my neighbor's front yard.

Now this fear would be one thing if she just got a little nervous when a cat was around, but it's turned into a major issue at our house. Every time my daughter sees the cat in the neighbor's front yard, she refuses to go outside. For example, yesterday when I needed to run to Target to grab a few things, I asked Nora to get her shoes on and hop into the car. She flat-out refused. She sat on the stairs and screamed and cried and refused to go. I finally dragged her outside and into the car kicking and screaming, which made for quite the fun drive to Target.

I don't want to ignore her fear—it seems genuine—but I also can't have her refusing to go outside anytime the kitten is in the yard.

What should I do?

Mike

Yep. Sounds just like Will. That fire alarm went off and he lost all ability to behave in the way he knew was right or rational. So while his fear was genuine, his reaction still had to be dealt with. Here's how I responded to Mike:

Dear Mike,

My friend's daughter is afraid of bees. To the point where if she sees a fly or an ant or a piece of black lint or anything else that could possibly resemble a bee, she panics and throws herself onto the ground.

Nora's fear of cats is a real fear: They scare her. They cause her not to think rationally and to respond incorrectly. That said, she can't behave incorrectly every time she sees something that scares her. So your job is twofold: Deal with the fear and help her to learn to control her behavior in spite of the feeling.

I have a few ideas that I think will help.

Erin

BIG PICTURE THEMES

- Fear
- Anxiety
- Disobedience
- Self-control

DISCIPLESHIP FOR A CHILD WHO IS STRUGGLING WITH FEAR

When I am afraid, I put my trust in you.

PSALM 56:3 (ESV)

Sadly, after the second fire alarm went off in the hotel, Will developed a very real and very adamant fear of all things fire related. Fire alarms, firefighters, fire trucks... oh, and real fires. Drat to that silly hotel fire alarm malfunction! The night of the alarm incident, he woke twice afraid the fire alarm would go off again. I had rubbed his back and reassured him that fires were rare and that if an alarm did go off, we knew how to get outside.

This continued after we got home from vacation. On the first night back, I heard the pitter-patter of little feet in the hallway at about eleven and Will climbed into bed with me. He was afraid the house would catch on fire. The next day we showed him our fire alarms and tested all of the batteries;

we showed him the routes he could take out of the house if the alarm did go off and practiced going to our family's safe outside meeting place. Yet that night, he ended up sleeping with his daddy and me again.

After several crying bouts by day when we spotted the neighborhood fire station that led to nights of fear (not to mention him kicking me all night, making it so none of us could sleep), I realized this was getting pervasive. So we decided that our new discipleship focus would be fear. Here's what we did:

- **Teach your child about courage.** In the Bible, God calls us—actually commands us—to have courage even when we are afraid. Joshua 1:9 says "Have I not commanded you? Be strong and courageous. Do not be frightened, and do not be dismayed, for the Lord your God is with you wherever you go." Talk to your child about how God calls us to be courageous even when we are afraid. With Will, since he was so young, we spent a lot of time talking about what he was afraid of (fires and monsters) and how he could overcome those fears with courage.

- **Read about warriors of faith.** Read Bible stories about men and women who overcame their fear and changed God's kingdom. *The Action Bible* (by Doug Mauss and Sergio Cariello) has a wonderful section entitled "A New Leader" based on the book of Joshua that really resonated with Will. We talked about how Joshua was scared to go into battle but how God went before him and led him to victory.

- **Fear not!** Isaiah 41:10 says, "Fear not, for I am with you." This is such a short, powerful reminder that our world is full of fear, but our world is also full of God. Even young kids—yes, even my five-year-old Will—can easily memorize this verse. We taught Will to say this verse himself whenever he feels the swell of fear in his heart and to remember that God is with him, protecting him. It has been very comforting.

- **Decorate with reminders.** I bought a couple of small chalkboards and wrote some favorite verses about fear on them. Then I drew little pictures—like one of a hand, one of a heart. I told Will that when he is scared at night, he can look at the pictures and remember the Bible verses we had read. The hand represented that Jesus always holds us tight in his hands. The heart means he loves us more than we could ever imagine.

PRACTICAL SOLUTIONS FOR A CHILD WHO IS STRUGGLING WITH FEAR

For God gave us a spirit not of fear but of power and love and self-control.

2 TIMOTHY 1:7 (ESV)

After the fifth or sixth night in a row with Will refusing to sleep in his own bed, I talked to my mom and she explained that she has found that often kids who struggle with fears have a disconnect between their understanding of what could happen and their emotional ability to deal with it.

Basically, our kids are too smart for their own good.

They recognize that something could hurt them—whether it's a fire that could burn the house down or a fierce kitten with fangs and claws—but they don't understand what to do with that recognition. So their heart rate rises, their breathing gets quick, and they start to panic, and they don't know how to emotionally cope with the fear.

These are genuine fear reactions—think of how you would feel when you were faced with some of your adult fears—with irrational triggers. I don't want to minimize the fact that kids are truly and honestly afraid.

The difference between children and (most) adults is that often adults' fears can't lead to poor choices. To help children behave rationally even when they feel afraid, we have to give them the tools they need to respond to their natural fears in a way that does not entail running into the street like a crazy person. Here are a few ideas:

1. Expose Your Child to His or Her Fear
Pillar: Growth

Before the hotel, Will knew plenty about fire safety. He knew that if a fire alarm went off, he had to get out of the building. He knew to find a safe outside meeting place. He knew to walk, not run, outside. But since his only experience with fire alarms was with drills—drills where his teacher had told him exactly what was coming before it happened—he had never experienced what it was like to respond to a fire alarm in the moment.

We had to change that.

At home, we showed Will how the fire alarm sounded and set it off. We practiced walking, not running outside to the tree (our safe meeting place). I even downloaded a fire safety app for him to play with to practice. At some point, we may actually set off the fire alarm in our house on purpose so he can experience what it is like to get outside unexpectedly, but I don't think he's ready for that yet.

No need to cause more sleepless nights with him in my bed.

Similarly, Mike needs to teach Nora all about cats. He could start by showing her pictures of kittens on the Internet or reading a few books about cats. Later, they could go to the animal shelter and look at cats and kittens from a distance. Maybe they could ask the neighbor about the white kitten. Find out its name. And when Nora is ready, maybe she could even pet the kitten with her father's supervision.

If your child's fear is something imaginary—like monsters or dragons—your strategy needs to be a bit different. Help your child to see that they are just pretend. Explain the difference between stories (read a few fictional books) and true events (read the Bible or a nonfiction book) and explain that monsters and dragons are stories. It's fine to check under the bed or in the closet each day or even to give your kid a flashlight to sleep with so they can shine it into the dark corners to check.

The more your child knows about their fear, the more likely they are going to be to respond rationally to that fear.

2. Give Your Child Emotional Coping Tools
Pillar: Growth

When kids don't know how to emotionally cope with their natural fears, they start to misbehave. This is why Nora refuses to put her shoes on and get in the car when the kitten is in the yard or why Will ran from the building screaming. Both kids needed emotional tools to help them respond right.

With Will, we asked him how he felt when the fire alarm went off. He explained that his head started to hurt really bad and his stomach felt like he was going to throw up. His gut reaction was to run to get away from that feeling. So we gave him some tools. For him, it was the phrase "stop, touch, and think"—if he started to have that feel-like-he-wants-to-throw-up feeling, he was to stop, touch his head, and then consider how he was supposed to respond. Once he had considered how he was supposed to respond, he would know that he shouldn't run if a fire alarm went off.

The same went for at night when he was worried about fires. He was supposed to stop—like tell the worries in his head to stop—and touch his head, and then think about the verse we had memorized: "Fear not, for I am with you." We told him to repeat that verse for as long as his stomach feels sick and then see if he can fall back asleep.

We did tell him that if he was still feeling sick or afraid after that process, to come find us. We didn't want him to feel like he couldn't seek out our help if he needed it, so we told him that we would always have a safe, warm, snuggly spot in our bed to come to if he really needed us.

3. Teach Your Child Not to "Water" Her Fears
Pillar: Desire

There's a great book called *What to Do When You Worry Too Much* by Dawn Huebner and Bonnie Matthews. In the book, worry and fear is equated to a tomato plant. The more you pay attention to it—watering it, feeding it, pruning it—the better it grows. The authors recommend that kids simply treat their fears like a tomato plant—to stop "watering" them (to take their thoughts captive, if you will)—and know that without "water," the fears will wither away and die.

We read this book to Will and told him he needed to stop "watering" his fear of fires. We told him to imagine his fear was a plant in the garden—he chose it to be a zucchini plant because he really doesn't like zucchini—and whenever his fear crept up, he should intentionally choose not to water it.

He told me he was imagining taking buckets of water and pouring them into the pool where he could swim so the zucchini plant got none. Take that, Zucchini! He told me he pictured the zucchini plant slowly dying and each time he thought about fires, he turned his thoughts to something else and didn't water the plant.

It worked.

Will hasn't been in our bed crying about fires for two months now. And he happily points out the fire trucks on the street when we drive by.

If we talk about fires, he still gets a little nervous, but the stomach-clenching, head-pounding fear is gone.

And I have decided not to serve any more zucchini with dinner.

OVERCOMING FEAR AND FINDING COURAGE

Kids naturally have fears.

When we teach them to respond appropriately to those fears, we show them what it means to take our thoughts captive and demonstrate self-control. We show them that regardless of that panicky, awful feeling they have in their stomachs, they can choose to respond correctly. Which hopefully means that the next time you see a tiny swim-trunk-clad boy running through the hotel parking lot, he will be on his way to the pool, safely holding his mama's hand.

―――――――

Dear Jesus,

You tell us in the Bible to "Fear not!" even as our human emotions are telling us to panic. Lord, help Will and Nora and each of us to press into You when we are scared. We have no reason to fear, for You are the Lord of this world and there is no fear, no emotion, no reaction that can separate us from Your love. Amen.

---- CHAPTER 16 ----

A Lukewarm Faith

(ELLEN)

Restore to me the joy of your salvation, and uphold me with a willing spirit.

PSALM 51:12 (ESV)

THE STRANGE THING ABOUT ELLA is that she really didn't rebel at all.

At least not in the expected ways.

Ella was a straight-A student who played the trumpet in the marching band and danced as Clara in the *Nutcracker* each Christmas. She was passionate and funny and the first person to volunteer to lead worship in her youth group. When she went off to college, everyone expected her to do great things.

And she did.

In college, she volunteered at a local dance studio to help preschoolers learn the basics of ballet. She entered the elementary education program and studied hard. She had great friends who played Monopoly and Life with her on Friday nights when others were out drinking. She even had a boyfriend—a shy boy named Daniel who wanted to be an engineer. They had made a vow to stay pure until they got married.

Yes, Ella was doing everything right.

Which is why it came as a complete shock to her parents when she came home for Christmas break and informed them that she had left the church. She explained that while she appreciated her faith-filled childhood, she was no longer a child and as part of her growing-up process she had become convinced that God was just a nice story. Talk about a surprise for her poor mom and dad!

The reason they hadn't seen it coming was because Ella had never been rebellious—and her about-face regarding God hadn't changed that. Ella wasn't drinking or doing drugs or dabbling in sexual promiscuity. She wasn't partying at the frat house or failing out of school. She wasn't dressing in tight clothes or sneaking out of their house at night. She was doing everything right in the eyes of the world.

And yet, she was doing it all wrong.

When I told my husband this story, he quickly nodded and explained that he understood. He, too, had grown up in a strong Christian home. He, too, had been brimming with head knowledge about who God is and what He stands for. And he, too, had gone off to college and drifted away from his faith.

Fortunately for my husband, God held fast to Glen and didn't let go. After a few years of fervent prayer and God's miraculous pursuit, Glen not only came back to God, but also came back to God with a renewed faith—a faith grounded in a heart-based passion for God instead of a simple knowledge of who God is.

Ella's parents had given Ella the knowledge she needed to follow God. But Ella's faith was lukewarm and wavering, and she never developed a passion for God in her soul. It's not too late—Isaiah 41:13 says that God holds his sons and daughters in the palm of his right hand. He doesn't let go. He doesn't toss us aside at our first waver. He holds fast.

No, it's not too late, but it is hard for Mom and Dad to bear. If this has happened to your son or daughter, hold fast to them just as Jesus will. Show them the power of God's love. Cling to God's promises. Pray that He will reveal Himself to them. Connect with them like you have never connected before. And while only God knows the state of each of our hearts, we can trust that He loves your child more than you do. And He will not let go.

Here's another story of a family struggling with a kid letting go of his faith:

Dear Ellen,

As a family, we have always gone together to church. It was our family routine to wake up on Sunday morning, have pancakes, head to church, and then go out to tacos at our favorite taco joint afterward. It was always a really special day for us—a time of worship, of communion, of learning and taking a Sabbath from the craziness of the rest of the week.

Notice I said "was" a special time. This fall, our son Jake, who is a sophomore in high school, told us that he would no longer be joining us. We asked him why and he simply said he isn't really into the whole church thing anymore. He admitted to us that he really just has no desire to pursue God. It's not that he doesn't believe in God anymore, but simply that he doesn't want to worry about Him anymore.

Obviously, this is much bigger than a "go-to-church-with-us-on-Sunday" conflict and I'm not quite sure how to navigate it. It's not like I can force him to be passionate about God or to pursue a relationship with God, but I also don't want to just sit back and say "fine" and let him slink away. I want him to have a vibrant, passionate faith.

What now?

Sincerely,
Kimberly

Kimberly is exactly right: Jake's problem is much bigger than not wanting to go to church. Jake clearly grew up in a loving, faith-nurturing environment where he was given the knowledge of God necessary to create a foundation of faith. But, unfortunately for Jake and many kids like him, that head knowledge hasn't quite translated to a heart passion. And that's where Kimberly needs to start. Here's how I responded to her:

Dear Kimberly.

First of all, I want to reassure you: All is not lost with your son. Yes, he's reached a point where he's not sure he wants to pursue God, but this isn't necessarily a bad thing. The reality is that the kids who never reach that point, kids who walk forward with a lukewarm faith and never grapple with what it means to be a Christian are the ones I worry about much more. So, as hard as it is, look at Jake's grappling as a good thing. It may take some time, but I am sure God is battling hard for Jake's heart. And rest assured: God's love for Jake is strong, fervent, and unwavering even as Jake wavers.

Resist the urge to go to either extreme with Jake. Do not force him to go to church with your family, but likewise, don't ignore his declaration and simply go without him. Instead, look at this as a key time to relate to him, to understand him, to connect with him, and to come to a place where he is ready to pursue God again.

A passionate pursuit of God starts with the head knowledge of who Jesus is and what He stands for, which is a foundation that I assume Jake already has. That knowledge is followed by passion. By a desire to be intimate with God, to follow Him without wavering. And that's that vision you must have for Jake. It will take work and intentional, connected parenting, but I believe that Jake's faith and desire to pursue God can ignite into a raging fire again.

Sincerely,
Ellen

BIG PICTURE THEMES

- Knowing God
- Connection
- Pursuit of holiness
- Sanctification

- Forgiveness
- Salvation
- Righteousness
- Passion

DISCIPLESHIP FOR KIDS WITH LUKEWARM FAITH

But in your heart honor Christ the Lord as holy, always being prepared to make a defense to anyone who asks you for a reason for the hope that is in you; yet do it with gentleness and respect.

I PETER 3:15 (ESV)

As a young child, I clearly remember walking in the clover fields that surrounded our country home, trying to wrap my mind around the concept of an eternal, infinite God. I would stand in the orchard and stare up into the sky, trying to imagine God and His universe, which extended infinitely. It was frightening to my young mind, sending my thoughts spinning wildly out of control. Try as I might, there was no way I could comprehend these incomprehensive thoughts.

Even as a small child, I sensed that while God was

unknowable, I still needed to seek to know Him. This was an interesting desire for a girl who was being raised in a home where no one read the Bible and where we never attended church. On Sundays, my mom would occasionally send my brothers and sisters and me down the hill to Sunday school in order to get us out of her hair. It was there where I learned that Jesus had died for my sins. I learned to regard Him as my Savior, but a distant, demanding, and judgmental one. This was an image that my finite mind could grasp.

Years later, in my sophomore year in college, I reached a point where I was really grappling with God. The God I had sought out in that clover field on our family farm was very different from the stern, eye-in-the-sky God I knew from Sunday school. I wasn't sure I really believed in him anymore. I wondered if it was just a childhood fairy tale that I was clinging to.

Then one day, a friend gave me a copy of A. W. Tozer's book *The Knowledge of the Holy*. That book became the catalyst for the renewal of my faith. As I read, I realized that my faith hinged upon what I considered to be true about God. At the time, the one attribute that seemed to resonate with me was His holiness. That fit with my view of God as being judgmental. He had every right to judge me, I reasoned, and to make demands of me. In light of His holiness, I despaired at my own failures and sin.

I did not yet know how to process my mistakes and failures with God and I was stuck there in my own pain. The guilt of my own sin became almost unbearable as I considered a holy God who stood against anything that degraded His holiness. I remember feeling utterly broken. In my brokenness, however, I was met by a loving, merciful, gracious God who wanted me to come to Him just as I was.

Yes, God pursued me even as I refused to pursue Him.

I had assumed that my weaknesses kept God away from me,

that because of His holiness, He would not associate with a sinner like me. But He met me tenderly one night as I lay prostrate before him, alone in my dorm room. He spoke to me through the story of Peter, who had returned to fishing after denying Jesus three times. How did Jesus respond? He came looking for Peter, who was restored once he realized that Jesus still wanted him. I realized that night that the holy God was also a tender, loving God. For the first time in my life, I felt peace and safety.

For our kids—especially those who struggle with doubt or ambivalence or a lack of passion—an understanding of who God is can help them feel that same peace and safety. The issue is: Are they willing to listen? Are they willing to discuss it with you? Oftentimes lecturing our kids about who God is does little when they, like me as a child, have misinformed perceptions or hardened hearts. So instead of telling our kids, we have to show them. Here are a few ideas:

- **Seek to understand the difference between knowledge, understanding, and wisdom.** Many kids who have a lukewarm faith are stuck in knowledge about God. They know the facts. They know what the Bible says. But they have never moved on to understanding or wisdom. Here are some quick biblical definitions:

  o **Knowledge** is about the facts. "An intelligent heart acquires knowledge and the ear of the wise seeks knowledge" (Proverbs 18:15).
  o **Understanding** is about translating meaning from the facts and applying it personally to one's life. It's about gaining discernment. "The unfolding of your words give light; it imparts understanding to the simple" (Psalm 119:130).

o **Wisdom** is about walking out what you know to be true—of allowing truth to define who you really are. "But the wisdom from above is first pure, then peaceable, gentle, open to reason, full of mercy and good fruits, impartial and sincere" (James 3:17).

Consider how you can move your kid past knowledge to understanding and more wisdom. Is it through more facts? Probably not. Instead, according to the Bible, it's about the unfolding of those facts into meaning and then allowing them to define who you are. Yikes! That's very heavy, I know, but I believe that the mistake parents make in this situation is that they focus so heavily on the facts—on drilling into their kids who God is and what He is—that they miss the opportunity to go deeper.

It says in James 3:17 that wisdom from above is first pure, then peaceable, gentle, open to reason, full of mercy and good fruits, impartial, and sincere. Can your conversations with your child be that? I think they can.

So open your household up to deep, wisdom-based conversation. Tell your child he can come to you at any point with questions, concerns, comments, doubts, or thoughts. Be willing to listen. Be willing to share your own journey of faith and your own struggles and doubts so that your child is able to see that he isn't alone in his feelings.

• **Challenge your kid to a book club.** Tell him that you will read any book that he chooses and in return, he has to read a book of your choosing and then the two of you can discuss it together. First, you need to read his book—willingly and excitedly. Then take him to coffee or frozen yogurt and talk about his book. Then it's your turn.

I recommend Tozer's *The Knowledge of the Holy* or C. S. Lewis's *Mere Christianity*. But those books can be pretty weighty, so if you think your kid would do better with an easier book, books like *The Case for Christ* would also work well. The key is to get your kid talking about things of faith and to be able to share your faith in a real, honest way.

- **Set up a family debate.** I have a grandchild or two who love to argue. Anyone else? Family debates work great for these types of kids, as they get to argue their own point—and they work great for kids who hate to listen, as they are forced to listen to other people's points as well. So give everyone in the family a question and give them some time to prepare their answer. Then get together and let each person stand for two minutes and explain their answer while the others listen. Then allow time for rebuttals and questions. Guide the conversation so it goes deep and gives your child room to really think about spiritual things in a new way. Oh, and make sure to make brownies or popcorn to serve as a post-debate treat. (Note: If you need family debate question ideas to get you started, I have a list of them posted under "resources" on my website, www.familywings.org.)

- **Become a servant leader.** In Mark 10:43 we learn that to be great, we must become servants. Apply that to your life, especially with your child who is struggling. Become a servant leader to him—show him what Christ's love really means. To be clear, I'm not telling you that you should wake up at four in the morning to bake him home-made cinnamon rolls and become his maid, but instead, seek to serve his needs as Christ would. Wash his feet, so to speak, by looking out for his spiritual and physical needs in a way that shows him what love really means.

PRACTICAL SOLUTIONS FOR KIDS WITH LUKEWARM FAITH

> *The Lord is not slow to fulfill his promise as some count slowness, but is patient towards you, not wishing that any should perish, but that all should reach repentance.*
>
> 2 PETER 3:9 (ESV)

The truth about God always has been and forever will be. He is unchanging. Unfailing. Unwavering. Which means that even as we as humans struggle with doubts or blips or changes in who we are, He remains the same. And so when our kids start to doubt God, it's important that we stay steady—unwavering and unchanging—in our belief about who God is and how He loves our kids.

Kids who struggle with God—who doubt their faith or let go of their heart passion for God—tend to omit attributes that they personally find offensive. Romans 1:22 is clear about what happens when we exchange the truth for a lie, when we claim to be wise ourselves and instead become fools. So how do we help our kids apply what they know about God to their lives? Here are a few ideas:

1. Spend Some Time Listening to Your Child
Pillar: Connection

As kids like Jake and Ella struggle to make sense of their faith, the worst thing their parents can do is lecture, nag, or force. Their words will fall on deaf ears and their hearts will harden even more. Instead, if your kid is struggling with faith, spend some time listening to him attentively, trying to understand his struggles.

Tell your child that you want to understand. Ask him to share with you his reasons, thought processes, and rationale.

Listen attentively and do not interrupt or give rebuttals for what he says. Pepper your speech with kindness and empathy, not condemnation. Listen. Give hugs. And listen some more.

As you listen to him tell you that he doesn't want to go to church anymore or participate in faith, make sure you extend him value by giving him the space to express what is really going on. Listen to his words and let him know that you love him no matter what and are not asking him to blindly accept your faith. Let him know that it's normal to grapple with faith at his age and that you would love to hear his questions and help him work through them. Be careful not to judge or push too hard but be calm and respect his need to question.

One caveat: Many parents associate listening with approval—that if they hear their kid's doubts and reasons, they are somehow approving of what they have to say. Honestly, there is a fine line between listening and approval. It's the same line that you have walked every day since he was born between being his parent and being his friend. I'm guessing you are a pro at that line by now! So as you listen, pepper your words with unconditional love, empathy, and respect. Don't argue or agree. But instead, go into this conversation with the goal of understanding where your child is coming from so that you will be able to approach his faith from an honest, wise place. One of the phrases I recommend saying is, "I hear you" because it's telling them that you've heard their words without necessarily agreeing with what they are saying.

2. Consider the Cover-Up
Pillar: Connection

The words kids say are often a cover-up for a real issue.

I see it all the time. A kid says she doesn't want to try out for the school play when really she wants it so badly and she's simply scared she might fail. A child says a friend has rejected him when really he knows the friend is making poor choices and he doesn't want to condone them. And a kid says he doesn't want to go to church with his family anymore because he's doubting God when really he is struggling with a hidden struggle or sin. Perhaps he is not relating with the youth pastor or other teens at church and that puts a damper on going on Sundays. Sadly, an all-too-common issue for teens is Internet porn, which takes over all other desires and snares them in a pit of shame and despair.

Your child's rejection of faith may be a desperate cry for help, and if you are too focused on getting him back into the church pew, you may miss that cry. So pause and prayerfully consider what could be going on. Ask questions. Dig deeper. And shower him with unconditional, unwavering love. Show him that while you may not approve of his choices, that no matter how deep of a hole he is in, you will always be there with a waiting hand to pull him out.

3. Share the Attributes of God without Lecturing
Pillar: Desire

When I grappled with my own faith, it was because I didn't truly understand God. I had learned in church that he was a just ruler and so I imagined him as a harsh, angry dictator who didn't truly love or care for me. I had to finally understand who He was to really deepen my faith. Of course, if you sit your kid down and start lecturing him about these things, he is likely to simply turn away. So consider ways you can share the attributes of who God is without lecturing.

Maybe you choose one attribute each day and discuss it over family dinner—including all family members in the conversation. Maybe you write an attribute on a chalkboard every week and leave it up for all to read and see. Or maybe you write the attributes in a shared family prayer journal and allow each family member to respond with their own thoughts and feelings. Some of these ways are passive—you may wonder if your lukewarm kid is even reading the notes you post on the chalkboard or the journal—but that's okay. The key here is kind, empathetic exposure. Not a forced lecture.

Share in the way that you think is best. And then pray. Pray that God will reveal Himself and His truth to your child in ways that you wouldn't expect. Pray that the words will touch his heart. And pray that his faith will ignite.

To get you started, here are a few points that I would start with:

- **God is self-sufficient.** Through him I am sufficient as well. Although he needs no one, yet He will work through anyone. "For the eyes of the LORD run to and fro throughout the whole earth to give strong support to those whose heart is blameless toward Him" (2 Chronicles 16:9 ESV).
- **God is all-wise.** I can rest in this and not fear. No matter how things look, all God does and allows is by His perfect wisdom. I need not trust in my own wisdom but in His infinite wisdom, because He is responsible for my eternal happiness and will manage the affairs of my life when I turn in faith to Him. "And we know that for those who love God all things work together for good, for those who are called according to His purpose" (Romans 8:28 ESV). "Trust in the LORD with all your heart; and do not lean upon your own understanding. In all your ways acknowledge Him, and He will make straight your paths" (Proverbs 3:5–6 ESV).

- **God is all-powerful.** Knowing this strengthens me. He both holds and sustains His creation in His hands. "Yours, O Lord, is the greatness and the power and the glory and the victory and the majesty, for all that is in the heavens and in the earth is yours. Yours is the kingdom, O Lord, and you are exalted as head above all. Both riches and honor come from you, and you rule over all. In your hand are power and might, and in your hand it is to make great and to give strength to all" (1 Chronicles 29:11–12 ESV).

- **God is sovereign.** He is all-knowing, all-powerful, and completely free to do what He wills. Yet, he has given me free will and authorized the law of choice. This seeming "contradiction" remains a mystery to me and beyond my finite comprehension. "Do not be deceived. God is not mocked, for whatever one sows, that will he also reap. For the one who sows to his own flesh will from the flesh reap corruption, but the one who sows to the Spirit will from the Spirit reap eternal life" (Galatians 6:7–8 ESV).

4. Inspire, Don't Force
Pillar: Desire

With younger kids, you can simply insist that they go to church. It's what you do as a family. However, once kids reach their teen years, it's harder to force them to go. I guess you could, but I'm also guessing that your child would get little from it when he arrived, and you would do little to grow his desire to go to church.

Essentially you have to let go of the reins and allow him to direct his own steps, all while wisely understanding he may not know where he is going. What a tough predicament! But it's doable. The key is inspiring in him a desire to pursue God on his own.

Make your focus about who you envision him becoming. Bring attention to his talents, strengths, and gifts. Note what makes him passionate. What are his dreams for his own life and what steps does he need to take to get there? What is going on in his life that prevents him from making progress toward his dreams? When our choices and actions don't line up with our dreams, we lose our way. Most importantly, let him know you are praying for him and that you are for him just as God is for him and not against him—that even doubts need not separate us from God's love.

INSPIRING A PASSIONATE FAITH

A bit of encouragement: I worry more about the kids who don't grapple with their faith at all, who don't ask the hard questions and push back a little than I do about kids like Jake and Ella. Because Ella's and Jake's struggle with faith means something important: They are searching.

They understand that faith is all or nothing. They understand that God wants everything and that in order to give God that, they have to buy in with their entire heart, mind, and soul.

And so take heart: God loves your child. He has him in the palm of His hand. And He wants his soul to belong to Him.

Pray hard, trust deeply, and be there for your kid, questions and all.

Because I am confident that God isn't done with either of them.

Dear Jesus,

We know that You are holding Jake in the palm of Your hand even as he grapples with big questions of faith. Lord, make Your presence clear to him and all of the other kids who are struggling with lukewarm faith. Ignite a fire in their hearts so that they will be passionate lovers of You. Amen.

LETTER TO THE READER

Dear Parents,

Thank you for joining us to put discipleship back into discipline. We pray that even as you face the struggles that are certain to pop up as you parent your kids, you'll find the grace to connect with your kids in a meaningful way through discipleship.

While we certainly haven't been able to address every discipline scenario that you will face, we pray that you will be able to find some tidbits to help you disciple your kids no matter what happens.

We believe that through careful, intentional discipleship, through connected conversation, and through a growth-forward vision, we can instill a desire to seek God and seek righteousness in our kids. It all starts with God's word—and how we can connect with our kids in a way that allows it to come to life in their hearts.

Please stay in touch with us through our websites (Erin at www.erinmacpherson.com and Ellen at www.familywings.org) and let us know how you are doing. And if you deal with a certain situation and your discipleship tactics work, please tell us about it! We'd love to learn and grow with you.

In Him,
Erin and Ellen

Acknowledgments

What a blessing to once again have the opportunity to share in the writing journey as a mother-daughter team! Over many full pots of coffee, we shed both tears and laughter as we contemplated raising kids and grandkids to love God and love family.

As with most books, this one happened with great help from our wonderful tribe. The incredible families we do school and life with at Veritas Academy shared stories and tips, thoughts and ideas. They also brought us meals, watched our kids, prayed for us, and cheered us on. Special thanks to Emily Deiss, Brenda Metro, Sarah Windham, Dina Morris, Mollie Burpo, Tara Hyde, Molly Ingram, Alison Morris, and Alysson Griffin, who each went out of their way to help us. We treasure your friendship.

Much thanks also to our respective agents, Steve Laube and Sarah Joy Freese, and to the editor on this book, Keren Baltzer, who has been a cheerleader, friend, and advocate for us. We so appreciate you.

And finally, our heartfelt appreciation and gracious thanks to our wonderful family, who buoys us with so much hope and love. Thank you Glen, Cameron, Troy, Stevi, Peter, and Alisa, plus Joey, Kate, Jude, Haddie, Greta, Will, Isaac, Asa, Elsie, Alma, and Beth—the adorable kids who give us so much writing fodder, not to mention incredible joy.

About the Authors

Erin MacPherson is the author of The Christian Mama's Guide series, the Hot Mama series, and *Free to Parent*. In addition to writing books, Erin cohosts the popular *So Here's the Thing* podcast with Kathi Lipp and stays busy speaking on the MOPS circuit, appearing on various radio shows and podcasts, and writing for magazines and publications like *Daily Guideposts*, *Thriving Family*, and *MomSense*. She is the mom to three young kids—Joey (age eleven), Kate (age nine), and Will (age five)—and is married to Cameron, who is an assistant principal at a big Texas public high school. Connect with Erin at www.ChristianMamasGuide.com or on Facebook at facebook.com/christianmamasguide.

Ellen Schuknecht is the author of *Free to Parent* and the forthcoming *A Spiritual Heritage*. Ellen and her husband of more than forty years, Glen, live in Austin, Texas, near their three adult children and their spouses, and their eleven grandchildren ranging in age from two to eleven. After spending more than forty years in education as a teacher, counselor, and school administrator, Ellen currently serves as the Family Ministries Director at Veritas Academy. She also currently cares for her eighty-eight-year-old mother, who is suffering with Alzheimer's. Check out Ellen's blog at www.FamilyWings.org.